REFORMED-CHARISMATIC WORSHIP

Its Theology and Practice

Other works by the author:

Deacons: Serving God, Serving God's People
A User's Guide to the Old Testament
Believe and Be Baptized

REFORMED-CHARISMATIC WORSHIP

Its Theology and Practice

Daniel J. Baker

Reformed-Charismatic Worship: Its Theology and Practice

Sovereign Grace Church
401 Upchurch St.
Apex, NC 27502
www.sgcapex.org

This revision completed March 28, 2015.

ISBN-13 978-1511489706
ISBN-10 1511489707

Acknowledging the Greatness of God

To the worship leaders and teams
of Sovereign Grace Church,
because you labor tirelessly and effectively
for the glory of Christ and the benefit of our people.
I love and respect you greatly.

CONTENTS

PART FOUR: SPECIFIC PRACTICES

INTRODUCTION

"Reformed-Charismatic" is...*what exactly?*

In the church we tend to either be labeled by our enemies or ourselves. In calling ourselves "Reformed-Charismatic" we are definitely choosing our own label. So what does it mean when we say *Reformed-Charismatic* worship? Parts One and Two of this book deals with the answer to that question, but it will be helpful to answer it more generally first. In fact, let's begin with the history behind it.

The "Reformed" part of the equation means that we identify ourselves with what took place in 16th century Europe in what is now called the Reformation. This was the birth of the Protestant church in many ways, though nothing was said in that century that did not have some connection to earlier schools of thought.

As the Reformation spread from Martin Luther in Germany throughout the countries of Europe the drumbeats were unmistakable: the unchallenged authority of the Word of God, which included submitting all doctrine and practice to its judgment; a renewed emphasis on conversion through faith in Jesus Christ; a passion to see the Scriptures taught clearly, read by all, and lived out as much as is possible. Other doctrines also seemed common among the Reformers. For instance, they often held to a view of God's sovereignty defined as his ordaining all things in our lives—whether circumstances or even our salvation. We identify with all of these understandings.

Calling ourselves "Charismatic" means we identify with a whole other movement within Christ's church, one with quite different distinctives. In 1906 in the Azusa Street revival in California, the Holy Spirit fell powerfully on a group of people and the event sent ripples throughout the country and even the world. Historians have called this the first of three "waves" of the Holy Spirit to hit the church in the twentieth century. Prophecy, tongues, healing, and the power of God to change lives was on display in an unprecedented manner—unprecedented in the recent history of the church.

The 1960's and 1970's saw a second wave of the Spirit move across the country and the world, predominantly through mainline denominations and even the Catholic Church. It was notable for its emphasis on speaking in tongues and the baptism of the Holy Spirit. Many movements that call themselves "non-denominational" were formed during this era.

In the 80's there was yet another dramatic move of the Spirit in what has been termed the Third Wave movement. Men like John Wimber and the Vineyard Movement are associated with this later move of the Spirit, and theologians such as Wayne Grudem identify themselves here. What was unusual about this wave of the Spirit was that it gained the support of many evangelicals. It also differed in its approach to the baptism of the Spirit, not seeing that a second and distinct "baptism of the Spirit" in Pentecost fashion was a requirement to be truly "filled with the Spirit."

These three waves of the Spirit differ on certain issues, but they are united in their expectation that God's Spirit works today just as he did in the first century church. What happened at Pentecost is unique historically and theologically, but not experientially. There is no gift described in the New Testament that does not have a continuing place in the church. In fact, it is only the return of Christ that makes gifts obsolete. This is "the perfect" that is to come, and "when the perfect comes, the partial will pass away" (1 Cor. 13:10).

We cannot, of course, identify with everything connected to the Reformation of the 16th century *and* the revivals of the 20th century. But here are three over-arching ideas that we associate with being "Reformed-Charismatic."

THE GOD WE WORSHIP

A first orienting idea we associate with being Reformed-Charismatic is how we define the God we worship. Here we are particularly influenced by the Reformers and those in their tradition. The Westminster Confession of Faith gives us one of many examples we could use to show the Reformers' exalted view of God:

> *There is but one only living and true God, who is infinite in being and perfection, a most pure spirit, invisible, without body, parts, or passions; immutable, immense, eternal, incomprehensible, almighty, most wise, most holy, most free, most absolute, working all things according to the counsel of His own immutable and most righteous will, for His own glory; most loving, gracious, merciful, long-suffering, abundant in goodness and truth, forgiving iniquity, transgression, and sin, the rewarder of them that diligently seek Him; and withal, most just, and terrible in His judgments; hating all sin, and who will by no means clear the guilty. (2:1)*

Such a high view of God affects our songs and all aspects of worship, because it will provoke us to capture the majesty and glory of our Creator and King. It inspires us to make our worship more about him than about us. It challenges us to be humble as we approach such a transcendent God. Lastly, it will mean that we are continually going back to the Scriptures to make sure that our worship is done in ways that please him; thus, there is a *continual Reformation* in the way that we worship.

HOW WE READ THE BIBLE

A second foundational idea is that the Reformers have taught us how to read our Bibles. To them the safest approach is summarized as *Scripture interprets Scripture* (or, *the analogy of faith*). This means that the best guide for interpreting the Bible is the Bible itself. If we are careful and patient readers of the Bible, it will give the necessary insights to interpret it correctly.

The most important aspect of this is that the New Testament is to guide how we read the Old Testament. The way that Jesus and the apostles understand God's Word acts as our interpretive grid for all of God's Word. Thus, we understand God's Word best by reading it *backwards*. The commands, history, and teaching of the Old Testament cannot be understood without the perspective of the New Testament. As one of many examples, Melchizedek is a shadowy figure when we encounter him in Genesis 14—until we read Hebrews 5-7.

Approaching our Bibles this way we see that Jesus Christ is not just the center of our New Testament, he is the centerpiece in all of Scripture (Luke 24:27; John 5:46; Rom. 1:1-4; etc.). We also see that the Bible unpacks for us a "history of redemption."[i] The Bible does not give us an exhaustive history of humanity from Adam to the new heavens and the new earth. World powers—Egypt, Assyria, Babylon, Greece, Rome—only enter the story as they impact the people of God. Even the people of God are not recorded exhaustively. Seth outlived Moses and David by five times *combined*, but gets only a few references in the Bible (e.g., 1 Chron. 1:1). The reason is that God presents for us the history *of redemption*, those events and people that impacted his unfolding work of redeeming his people.

A third conviction about our Bible flows out of the first two, namely, that while the old covenant has been replaced by the new (Hebrews 8), the Old Testament still provides a rule of life for the Christian. Its moral commands still speak to the Christian, calling for our obedience as understood through the lens of the redemption of Christ. We believe this because this is the apostolic example we find in places like Ephesians 4:25, Romans 12:19-20, 1 Peter 1:16 and 3:10-12, and Hebrews 3:7-11.

This is a complicated issue, but it touches significantly on worship because of the book of Psalms. Do the Psalms command us in particular ways with respect to our worship? If the Old Testament no longer binds us, then it provides only indirect examples and encouragements. But if the Psalms still command us in our worship, then when it says "clap your hands" (47:1) and "sing a new song" (144:9) and "praise him with trumpet sound" (150:3), we must obey. For us, the Psalms as well as the entire Old Testament are contained in Paul's assessment: "*All Scripture* is breathed out by God and profitable for teaching, for reproof, for correction, and for training in righteousness, that the man of God may be complete, *equipped for every good work*" (2 Tim. 3:16-17, emphasis mine).

THE SPIRIT OF PENTECOST

A third idea that undergirds this whole work is that God's Spirit works in us today in all the ways we see described and taught in the New Testament. The Spirit that is poured out at Pentecost is for "the last days" (Acts 2:17ff.), not just that day. The result of God pouring out his Spirit is the gospel advancing and the church being established (Acts 2:42-47; 4:29-31; 8:4-25). It is also the power of the Spirit displayed in gifts given to men and women that enable them to minister to one another, to unbelievers, and to God himself (Rom. 12:3-8; 1 Cor. 12-14; Eph. 4:11-16; 1 Peter 4:9-10; etc.). These gifts are to have a place in the life of the believer and especially in the corporate worship of the church (e.g., 1 Cor. 14:26). All of this will be explored in our chapter on spiritual gifts.

The God we worship, our approach to the Bible, and the role of the Holy Spirit in our church life: This is some of what we mean by "Reformed-Charismatic." These insights ground all that is said in coming chapters of our discussion.

IT'S...COMPLICATED AND SIMPLE

In the pages ahead we will traverse some rugged terrain. This is unavoidable when we deal with something as vast and significant as worship. Right now maybe worship for you is a simple event where you express your love to Jesus Christ purely for his pleasure. Nothing that we will say ahead is meant to change that. Lord willing, when all is said and done, your worship will remain just as simple and sincere, but hopefully it will also grow in its depth and breadth and in your ability to lead others in proclaiming the all-surpassing glory of God.

NOTES

[i] Or "salvation history." Some authors have taken to using the phrase, "The Storyline of the Bible," and by this they mean that while the Bible contains 66 books, really there is a single, over-arching story that connects everything we find there. This story has a "storyline," which is the story of God accomplishing his redemption.

PART ONE

A Theology of Worship

CHAPTER ONE

Proclaiming the All-Surpassing Glory of God

CONFUSED IN WONDERLAND

In Lewis Carroll's *Through the Looking Glass,* Alice has an infamous conversation with Humpty Dumpty that is prescient for our discussion about *Reformed-Charismatic* worship:

> *'That shows that there are three hundred and sixty-four days when you might get un-birthday presents—*
>
> *'Certainly,' said Alice.*
>
> *'And only one for birthday presents, you know. There's glory for you!'*
>
> *'I don't know what you mean by "glory,"' Alice said.*
>
> *Humpty Dumpty smiled contemptuously. 'Of course you don't—till I tell you. I meant "there's a nice knock-down argument for you!"'*
>
> *'But "glory" doesn't mean "a nice knock-down argument,"' Alice objected.*
>
> *'When I use a word,' Humpty Dumpty said in rather a scornful tone, 'it means just what I choose it to mean—neither more nor less.'*
>
> *'The question is,' said Alice, 'whether you can make words mean so many different things.'*

> *'The question is,' said Humpty Dumpty, 'which is to be master - - that's all.'*
>
> *Alice was too much puzzled to say anything, so after a minute Humpty Dumpty began again. 'They've a temper, some of them -- particularly verbs, they're the proudest -- adjectives you can do anything with, but not verbs -- however, I can manage the whole of them! Impenetrability! That's what I say!'*
>
> *'Would you tell me, please,' said Alice 'what that means?'*[i]

Lewis Carroll is playing with us, but he is also instructing us. His point might have more to do with linguistic theories that deconstruct meaning in communication (to put some current labels to it), but he also makes a point germane to us. "Worship" means something different to virtually everyone who uses the term. We need to think carefully to make sure that our use of the term accords with the Bible's teaching on the subject. Traditions, experience, and personal preference often control the meaning of this word more than the Bible itself. So, for this chapter we will examine it more closely and hopefully answer Alice's question, *"Can you tell me, please, what that means?"*

"WORSHIP" IN HEBREW AND GREEK

Searching in our English Bibles on "worship" shows that the term is found almost 200 times. Behind this English word in most cases is the Hebrew word *chavah*[ii] or the Greek word *proskuneō*. Combined they are used about 232 times in our Bibles in ways that overlap significantly. Both can be translated as the more literal "bowing down" or the more comprehensive term "worship."

The Hebrew *chavah* first occurs in Genesis 18:2 where Abraham meets the Lord and "bowed himself to the earth." He bows because he has a sense that the one before him is superior to him. It is no mere formality at work here. It is a bowing down which implies respect and reverence. Indeed, in many places it is far more than a general show of respect we might pay to another person (cf. Gen. 23:12), but is a bowing down before deity. We see this in Leviticus 26:1 where Israel is commanded *not* "to bow down" to an idol or graven image.

The term can also mean "worship" in a general sense without specifically implying that someone is "bowing down." We see this in Exodus 24:1 when Moses, Aaron, and the elders are to come up to the LORD and "worship the Lord from a distance." In Nehemiah 9:6 the supremacy of our God is seen by the fact that even "the host of heaven worships you."

This word is often used in places that are warning Israel against false worship, as in the second commandment: "You shall not *bow down* to them or serve them, for I the LORD your God am a jealous God" (Ex. 20:5). Israel's idolatry breaks out, however, as they build the golden calf and then "worshiped it and sacrificed to it" (Ex. 32:8).

The Greek word *proskuneō* has a similar range of meaning.[iii] Bauer's lexicon says the verb is actually two roots joined together, one of them meaning "to kiss." There is nothing romantic in this word, however, for it is "frequently used to designate the custom of prostrating oneself before persons and kissing their feet or the hem of their garment, the ground, etc." Such displays and others were "to express in attitude or gesture one's complete dependence on or submission to a high authority figure."[iv]

At times the word refers to a literal "bowing down" in the gospels when someone comes before Jesus and "bows down." The "leper" bows before Jesus and pleads for healing (Matt. 8:2), and the ruler bows before Jesus on behalf of his daughter (Matt. 9:18). This bowing down is no mere politeness, however, and clearly communicates that the one in need sees Jesus as the powerful and superior one.

The term means the more comprehensive "worship" with the wise men in Matthew 2. They see the baby Jesus as the one "born king of the Jews" and desire to offer their worship to him (vv. 2, 8, 11). In John's gospel we have the critical encounter between Jesus and the woman at the well in chapter three. Nine times in five verses John uses *proskuneō* or cognates. Jesus says that true "worship" is currently found among the Jews in

Jerusalem and not in Samaria, but an "hour is coming" when true worship shall not be tied to a place at all, but it will be "in spirit and in truth" (4:21-24). In Revelation there are many times when people "fall down" before God (5:14), but when *proskuneō* is used it typically means the more general "worship," as when the angel tells John, "Worship God" (19:10).

What do these two words say about worship?

PROCLAIMING THE ALL-SURPASSING GLORY OF GOD

These two ways the Hebrew and Greek words are used points us toward the essence of all worship. The physical act of bowing down merely expresses what is in view when the more general side of worship is implied. Worship, then, is *proclaiming the all-surpassing glory of God.* No verb can fully capture the whole array of words that depict the soul's awareness of and recognition of and response to the glory of God, a glory that transcends and surpasses all things, but "proclaim" points us in the right direction. It is a proclamation that starts within our being and involves our thoughts, motivations, words, praises, and even our very lives.

Proclaiming the all-surpassing glory of God looks different at different times. A soul buried under grief and temptation proclaims his glory by the simple act of saying, "Lord, amidst it all I remember that you are worthy and great." This is the kind of worship offered by Jesus in Gethsemane. Yet, proclaiming his glory can also include choirs and trumpets and shouts and songs and look a lot like what we read in Psalm 150, "Let everything that has breath praise the LORD!" (v. 6).

What we proclaim is God's *all-surpassing glory*. This, too, is a summary which points to all that God is and does. Thus, worship is proclaiming his infinitude and grace and love and mercy and power and omnipresence and holiness and splendor and salvation and righteousness and redemption and omniscience and wisdom and knowledge and all the works he does to reveal these attributes.

In saying it is *all-surpassing* I mean that worship does far more than proclaim that God is a little bit of this or that, or that he is a little more this or that. Worship is proclaiming that he is unmatched, unrivalled, unparalleled, and singularly great in all of his attributes. We are worshiping a God who has no rival in any way whatsoever. This also means he infinitely surpasses every situation and problem and sin and temptation and obstacle that we will face. Before cancer and bankruptcy and unemployment and terrorism and global warming, we can still proclaim his all-surpassing glory.

The English word "worship" has such a sense to it. In its Old English heritage it was a combination of "worth" meeting the suffix "-ship," which means ascribing worth to something.[v] Biblical worship is simply ascribing worth to our glorious God who has revealed himself in creation, scripture, and through the Holy Spirit. Authors such as Jerry Bridges think of worship along these lines. He says, "This is the essence of worship: Ascribe to the Lord the glory due His name."[vi]

Of course, such a proclamation does not begin with us. It must begin with God himself. He is the one who makes worshipers. Many authors include this notion in their definition of worship. As an example, John Stott says,

> *All true worship is a response to the self-revelation of God in Christ and Scripture, and arises from our reflection on who He is and what He has done....The worship of God is evoked, informed, and inspired by the vision of God....The true knowledge of God will always lead us to worship.*[vii]

Thus, when Jesus says that "the Father is seeking such people to worship him" (John 4:23), we are reminded that God's work is primary and our response is secondary. He is doing all of the internal work in our hearts so that we will offer true worship to him.

PROCLAIMING HIS GLORY IN PSALM 99

In Psalm 99 we have a vivid example of someone smitten by God's all-surpassing glory who is then calling all people to respond in worshiping him (vv. 5, 9). Note how the attributes of God evoke worship in this psalm:

The LORD reigns;
let the peoples tremble!
He sits enthroned upon the cherubim;
let the earth quake!
2 The LORD is great in Zion;
he is exalted over all the peoples.
3 Let them praise your great and awesome name!
Holy is he!
4 The King in his might loves justice.
You have established equity;
you have executed justice and
righteousness in Jacob.
5 Exalt the LORD our God;
worship at his footstool!
Holy is he!

6 Moses and Aaron were among his priests,
Samuel also was among those
who called upon his name.
They called to the LORD,
and he answered them.
7 In the pillar of the cloud he spoke to them;
they kept his testimonies and the statute
that he gave them.
8 O LORD our God, you answered them;
you were a forgiving God to them,
but an avenger of their wrongdoings.
9 Exalt the LORD our God,
and worship at his holy mountain;
for the LORD our God is holy!
(Ps. 99:1-9)

God's glory—his holiness, forgiveness, mercy, transcendence, power, and righteousness—and our worship are unmistakably connected here. We "exalt" and "worship" him as the only right response to his revealed glory. Worship here is merely giving voice to the sense of God's all-surpassing glory felt by the psalmist. The God he worships is great above all people, all creation, all beings. He alone is to be exalted as "the LORD our God," because he alone "is holy" (v. 9). Our worship might be tearful or joyful, silent with grief or exploding with songs, expressed in a choir or in faithful parenting, but to be worship it must possess some attempt to capture the surpassing glory of God.

SUNDAY AND EVERY DAY

To understand worship in this way will make every moment a potential moment of worship. A worship team and a church building are not required to proclaim God's unrivalled greatness. I do this when I am cut off in traffic and because of my awareness of his supremacy over me, I choose not to be angry. I do this when I am wrestling with fatigue and yet because of my sense that God is worthy, I wake up to pray and read the Bible. I worship when I am faced with temptation, but because of my recognition that God is infinitely wonderful, I choose obedience instead.

In other words, this understanding connects worship to the whole rest of our Christian lives. As we will see in the next chapter, all of our obedience, sacrifice, and praise can be worship when we do it as a proclamation of the all-surpassing glory of God. That is where we must now turn.

NOTES

[i] Lewis Carroll, *Through the Looking Glass,* originally 1871 (Forgotten Books, 2008), 66-67.

[ii] When this root refers to "worship" it is found in a form that grammarians have called "hishtaphel," one relatively rare for other verbs. The close tie between this specific root and its unusual form prompts some grammarians to give it "extraordinary cultural significance" (Waltke, O'Connor, 361). There is another root spelled the same way but not found in this form that means "life, living."

[iii] Further, it is also the main Greek word used in the Septuagint (Greek Old Testament of the second and third centuries BC) to translate *chavah.* Thus, this term is more-or-less the definitive Greek term for the early Christians to speak about "worship."

[iv] Frederick William Danker, ed., *Greek-English Lexicon of the New Testament and Other Early Christian Literature, 3rd ed.* (Chicago, IL: The University of Chicago Press, 2000).
[v] *Webster's Ninth New Collegiate Dictionary* (Springfield, MA: Merriam-Webster Inc., 1987).
[vi] *The Joy of Fearing God* (Colorado Springs, CO: Water Brook Press, 1999), 235. For similar definitions see Wayne Grudem, *Systematic Theology* (Grand Rapids, MI: Zondervan, 1994), 1003; John Frame, *Worship in Spirit and Truth* (Phillipsburg, NJ: P&R Publishing, 1996), 1.
[vii] *The Message of Romans,* The Bible Speaks Today (Downers Grove, IL: InterVarsity Press, 1994), 311. For similar definitions see Allen Ross, *Recalling the Hope of Glory* (Grand Rapids, MI: Kregel Publications, 2006), 50; D.A. Carson, *Worship by the Book* (Grand Rapids, MI: Zondervan, 2002), 26.

CHAPTER TWO

Worship Expressed through Obedience, Sacrifice and Praise

The last chapter explored what worship *is*. This chapter looks at what worship *does*. For worship to be truly worship it must proclaim the unmatched glory of God, but for worship to be truly worship it must also result in actually doing something. The idea of worshiping without any expression of that worship is just as nonsensical as saying you love someone without giving any expression of it. It is words, actions, and thoughts that demonstrate love to be truly love.

Biblical worship has three sides to it, which are inseparable and which hit on a key aspect of what worship does: obedience, sacrifice, and praise. All of these must be biblically defined to be biblical worship, of course, but we will see that whether it is in the Old or New Testament, whether under the old covenant or the new, whether in the tabernacle or the gathered church, whether privately or corporately, worship is expressed by obedience, sacrifice, and praise. In fact all of the later discussions on the components of corporate worship (chapter four) or the Lord's Supper (chapter six) are merely applications of this obedience, sacrifice, and praise.

WORSHIP EXPRESSED THROUGH OBEDIENCE

The first and perhaps most important expression of our worship is obedience. It is vital to grasp this connection between worship and obedience. The notion that we can worship God and not obey him is foreign and repugnant to the biblical writers. Those who sing the loudest and make bold statements about their sacrifices for the Lord get the sternest rebukes when this is not connected to a life of obedience. God rebukes Israel harshly for living sinfully but continuing their public worship: "I hate, I despise your feasts, and I take no delight in your solemn assemblies" (Amos 5:21). Why such harsh words? Because "justice" and "righteousness" (v. 24) had no place in the hearts and lives of the worshipers. Their worship became a mere show, the epitome of hypocrisy. Our worship must be expressed by a life of obedience if it is to be true worship.

When the Bible speaks of our worship through obedience it does so by the expression, "serving the Lord." Often "worship" and "serve" are used together in such a way that they are really two terms speaking of the same larger response to God. Jesus himself speaks in this way when he rebukes the devil: "You shall worship (*proskunēseis)* the Lord your God and him only shall you serve (*latreuseis*)" (Matt. 4:10). "Worship" and "serve" are often joined when speaking of false worship, or the worship of gods other than the true God: "Take care lest your heart be deceived, and you turn aside and serve other gods and worship them" (Deut. 11:16; cf. Deut. 8:19; 1 Ki. 9:6; Jer. 13:10; Rom. 1:25). It is clear that we cannot separate serving God from worshiping God. To commit ourselves to biblical worship is to commit ourselves to biblical obedience.

At other times "service" is seen as the whole response we give to God. In Exodus 3:12 the Lord tells Moses, "I will be with you, and this shall be the sign for you, that I have sent you: when you have brought the people out of Egypt, you shall serve God on this mountain." Which mountain? Mt. Sinai. Yes, the very mountain on which God gave the Law and the instructions for the tabernacle, on which he met with the seventy elders who saw him. All of that fiery glory which they would behold. All of the detailed instruction about the tabernacle and the priesthood. All of that is summarized in Exodus 3:12 as Israel "serving" the Lord. For centuries they had "served" Egypt, but God was saving them to serve him alone (Ex. 1:13).

Paul himself speaks in similar terms when he calls God the one "whom I serve with my spirit in the gospel of his Son" (Rom. 1:9). He will tell Felix the governor, "I serve the God of our fathers, believing everything that is in accordance with the Law" (Acts 24:14, NASB). He also speaks of the Thessalonians and how they "turned to God from idols to serve the living and true God" (1 Thess. 1:9). Our redemption is "so that we [can] serve in the new way of the Spirit and not in the old way of the written code" (Rom. 7:6). All of this means that we are to join with Jesus in saying, "My food is to do the will of him who sent me and to accomplish his work" (John 4:34). Thus, we worship through our service.

Worship itself is a kind of service also as we remember that we are commanded to give him worship. When we obey the command of Scripture, "Sing praises to the LORD, who sits enthroned in Zion" (Ps. 9:11), we are offering to him worship, but this is also serving him because it is done according to his Word.

This service is no mere duty, certainly no drudgery. To emphasize the obedience aspect as we have might make it sound like performing external and sad-faced acts is enough. It is not. Service is to be the overflow of a heart that worships God.

We are to offer "acceptable service with reverence and awe" (Heb. 12:28, NASB). "Reverence and awe" takes our actions of "service" and makes them "acceptable." That is, they go from being lifeless and potentially hypocritical actions to being true worship.

And as we said, "service" is always to be directed to the true God. In Deuteronomy 8:19 Moses warns Israel that "if you forget the LORD your God and go after other gods and serve them and worship them, I solemnly warn you today that you shall surely perish" (cf. also 11:16; 30:17; Jer. 13:10). Service is to be reserved for the true and living God.

We should be careful here that we do not dismiss such warnings. The false gods that we worship rarely come in the form of totem poles or gold statues. Our gods do not have foreign names like Balaam or Molech or Jupiter or Zeus. Instead, we "go after other gods and serve them and worship them" when we elevate something other than God in our hearts to such an extent that we "serve" it. Maybe my god is the appearance of success. I "serve" such a god by working tireless hours to get money to afford the status symbols of our day—a bigger house, a nicer car, a better vacation. Maybe my god is comfort. I "serve" this god by making sure that my house is always 72 degrees, I always have my beverage of choice in my hand, my kids are always quietly playing *somewhere else*, and I always have my favorite book in hand. The gods that I serve at such times have non-offensive names like pleasure, peace, comfort, reputation, success, fame, security, or respect. God wants me to set all of these aside and serve him: "You shall worship the Lord your god and him only shall you serve" (Mat. 4:10).

WORSHIP EXPRESSED THROUGH SACRIFICE

The second key expression of our worship is sacrifice. The author of Hebrews writes,

> *Through him then let us continually offer up a sacrifice of praise to God, that is, the fruit of lips that acknowledge his name. Do not neglect to do good and to share what you have, for such sacrifices are pleasing to God. (13:15-16)*

The author of Hebrews spends much time in his letter working through the old covenant sacrifices and how they are fulfilled in the cross of Christ. Yet, he does not see the cross as the end of sacrifice; it merely brings a profound change to our sacrifices. Now we offer "praise to God, that is, the fruit of lips that acknowledge his name," and this is sacrifice. We "do good and…share what [we] have," and this is sacrifice. These are sacrifices "pleasing to God." Good works and worship are the sacrifices that we offer as Christians, and these continue even into the new heavens and new earth.

In the Old Testament we see more literal sacrifices offered as acts of worship. After his deliverance from the flood, Noah "built an altar" and made a sacrifice, one that pleased the Lord (Gen. 8:20ff.). He offered burnt animals to communicate his sense of gratitude and humility to the God who had just delivered him from a global flood of destruction. This was an act of worship for Noah.

Abraham builds altars throughout his life in response to the grace he experiences from the Lord. Thus, after his initial call from the Lord, he journeys to Canaan and is there promised the land. In response to the promise of God, he "built there an altar to the LORD, who had appeared to him" (Gen. 12:7). He builds an altar and calls "upon the name of the LORD" when he journeys east of Bethel (12:8). In Hebron he will build an altar (13:18). He will also build an altar on Mt. Moriah where he is commanded to take his only son "and offer him there as a burnt offering" (22:2, 9). Of course, the Lord provides a ram to offer in his place. Animals are also offered in 15:9 when the covenant is made. The altar-making worship of Abraham will be duplicated by Isaac and Jacob as well (Gen. 26:25; 33:17ff; 35:1-7).

Such offerings are never connected to sin. Instead, they are made for thanksgiving and worship. These men did something costly for the Lord to show him they were aware of his great work in their lives. Building an altar took time, and offering livestock cost them money. These animals were their livelihood. To offer them was a statement before God that he was more valuable to them than whatever profits the animals might gain them in the years to come.

SACRIFICE IN THE LAW OF MOSES

With the first Passover in Exodus 12, the frequency and variety of sacrifices increases dramatically under Moses. They also become a central part of how the people of God relate to him. The people of God from the Exodus onwards deal with God through an intricate and comprehensive system of sacrifices.

In Exodus 12 the Lord commands Israel to offer the Passover lamb and to spread the blood of this lamb on their doorposts. The angel of death that would kill the firstborn of all in Egypt would "pass over" any door that had this blood upon it. Forever afterwards this Passover was to be celebrated annually in

Israel and was to be the start of their year. It thus became a sacrifice to mark God's deliverance from their bondage to Egypt.

Sacrifices were offered at the "Feast of Weeks" seven weeks later to celebrate God's provision of their crops (Deut. 16:9ff.). Their cycle of feasts ended with the Day of Atonement in the seventh month (Lev. 16), a festival explicitly about sin. "And this shall be a statute forever for you, that atonement may be made for the people of Israel once in the year because of all their sins" (16:34). Other offerings are made as "peace offerings for thanksgiving" (Lev. 7:13ff.), for the Sabbath (Lev. 23:11ff.), to consecrate men as priests (Ex. 29:21), and to inaugurate a covenant (Ex. 24:8). There are many others besides.

The sheer expense of these offerings is staggering, and some estimate that it constitutes as much as 20% of their annual income. These sacrifices also remind us that God has a claim on our entire life. No part of our lives is outside of his lordship. He has total ownership of us.

Yet, we should not imagine that God only cared about their physical sacrifices. In the Psalms we find verses like 51:17, "The sacrifices of God are a broken spirit; a broken and contrite heart, O God, you will not despise." And Amos 5:22 says that "though you offer me your burnt offerings and grain offerings, I will not accept them," because they were not joined to a broader life of obedience.

These verses make it clear that God was looking for a heart of worship behind these offerings. They were to be an expression of worship and not Pharisaic acts of duty. Thus, when God was in view with all of his greatness and mercy, he was shockingly tolerant of their sins (e.g., think of King David). When God was not in view and sacrifices were showy displays of pride and self-importance, he would not even tolerate their offerings. Nadab and Abihu, remember, were killed while offering their sacrifice (Lev. 10:1-3). In other words, it is tragic to separate our sacrifices from our worship.

THE SACRIFICE OF CHRIST AND...ME

Of course, we read of these sacrifices as Christians and not Old Testament saints. That means we need to read them through the lens of the cross of Christ. Through the cross Jesus fulfilled what all the blood of animals could never fulfill. He "once for all" offered his own blood, "thus securing an eternal redemption" (Heb. 9:12). His sacrifice means that no other animals need ever be killed in the worship of God or to atone for sin or to cleanse the people of God.

His sacrifice also brought an end to worship rooted in the temple of God (John 2:13-22; 4:21-24). Worship is now "in Spirit and truth" and not in the temple of Jerusalem by the law of Moses. No longer is the priesthood required for access to God. No longer is the language of our worship and thanksgiving spoken through drink and grain and animal sacrifices. His sacrifice has brought an end to all such ceremonies found in the law of Moses. Yet, does this mean the end of all sacrifice? Absolutely not.

It is true that the New Testament speaks clearly that animal sacrifice has ended, but this does not mean the end of all sacrifice, however. Now what we sacrifice is...ourselves. We can see this in at least three ways.

First, we offer ourselves as living sacrifices. Paul says in Romans 12:1, "I appeal to you therefore, brothers, by the mercies of God, to present your bodies as a living sacrifice, holy and acceptable to God, which is your spiritual worship." Paul is by no means calling for the meager offering of an animal. He is instead appealing that our very lives be given to the Lord "as a living sacrifice." Because it is "living" it is ongoing. It does not end. A sacrificed animal dies in the process, never to hunt or eat or plough again. A "living sacrifice" is meant to live a life of continual sacrifice.

Second, we offer ourselves by serving others: "Even if I am to be poured out as a drink offering upon the sacrificial offering of your faith, I am glad and rejoice with you all" (Phil. 2:17). The "drink offering" was part of the sacrificial system of Moses, a small addition to many sacrifices. Paul is seeing his own life as "poured out" in this sense, a cup full which is to be made empty for a greater cause. The cup pours something out which is lost upon the ground forever, never to return to the cup. The cup cannot fight for its own contents and pour them out for others simultaneously. Paul sees his work on behalf of "your faith" as such an offering. His labor is not in vain, for it is for the sake of a mature faith in these Philippians. Thus, our service for others is a sacrifice that we gladly make.

Third, we offer sacrifices by offering praises: "Through [Christ] then let us continually offer up a sacrifice of praise to God, that is, the fruit of lips that acknowledge his name" (Heb. 13:15). All sacrifice for sin is fulfilled in Jesus, but we see here that there is another sacrifice that will never be fulfilled, the "sacrifice of praise to God." Instead of altars and animals, it is now our words and songs and speech—"lips that acknowledge his name"—that make these offerings.

This offering of ourselves becomes worship when God is in view. Otherwise we run the risk of doing good works for our own reputation (self-centeredness) or to satisfy our own sense of righteousness (self-righteousness) or to make up for what we think the cross lacked (self-atonement). None of this will do. Instead we are to lay down our lives in obedience to Christ as we joyfully acknowledge his claim on our lives and his surpassing worth above all things. In fact, one of the ways we will know that we are giving him worship is that we will be able to join with those saints who testify, "I never made a sacrifice." They don't mean they never suffered hardship or loss or pain or suffering. They mean that when all is weighed in the balance and these losses are compared to the glory of knowing Christ, we can attest with Paul: "I count everything as loss because of the surpassing worth of knowing Christ Jesus my Lord" (Phil. 3:8).

WORSHIP EXPRESSED THROUGH PRAISE

So, worship is expressed through obedience, and it is also expressed through sacrifice. Now we see that worship is also expressed through praise. This mirrors most closely what we often call "worship" in our Sunday services—the songs, corporate prayers, instruments, choirs, processions, calls to worship, etc. This is also the most distinctly outward of the expressions of worship. We can be quietly aware of God's greatness, silently obedient to his word in our service, or making the anonymous sacrifices that Christians often make. Yet, to be internally praising the Lord is almost a contradiction in terms. It would be like silently talking or internally shouting. Praise must be expressed! Thus, when David brought the ark to Jerusalem and the city is aware of what this means, there is not silent reflection. There is praise: "The people said, 'Amen!' and praised[i] the LORD" (1 Chron. 16:36).

Praise is found in both the Old and New Testaments, literally from Genesis (29:35) to Revelation (19:5). The occurrences in the Old Testament dwarf those in the new, but this has to do with the book of Psalms, a book filled with all manner of praises.

As we reflect on the Old Testament teaching on praising God we should note that this is a place where the redemptive work of Christ changes our interpretation very little. While it is true that the tabernacle/temple itself has no place for new covenant saints, this does not mean that we do away with all that pertains to the tabernacle/temple. Prayer is one of the more obvious examples. Prayers were lifted up in the tabernacle/temple (2 Chr. 30:27), but we are also to "pray without ceasing" (1 Thess. 5:17). Likewise, praise was lifted up in the temple (1 Chr. 16:4), and we are also to praise our God (Heb. 13:15). Jesus changes our understanding of the God we are praising and gives us a glorious new redemption to praise him for, but by no means do the praises (with choirs and instruments and all that is included in Davidic worship) end in the new covenant. We will therefore look at praising God primarily through the lens of the book of Psalms.[ii]

PSALM 150

Psalm 150 is the last one in the Psalter, and yet it provides a wonderful overview of praise for the believer. It is one of the "Hallelujah" psalms (146-150). All of these begin and end with the Hebrew *hallelujah* which means literally, "Praise the LORD!", a combination of the root *halal* ("praise") and *–yah*, a suffix that means Yahweh. Psalm 150 has thirteen occurrences of the word "praise" in its six short verses and thus provides a mini-theology for the whom, where, why, and how of our praise.

We learn *whom* we are to praise in the opening *hallelujah*: "Praise the LORD!" (v. 1a). Only the true and living God is worthy of the praises of his people. We also learn *where* we are to praise him: "Praise God in his sanctuary; praise him in his mighty heavens" (v. 1b). For the Christian who understands the fulfillment of Christ, this means that we praise him "in spirit and truth" (John 4:21-24).

Psalm 150 also tells us *why* we are to praise him: "Praise him for his mighty deeds; praise him according to his excellent greatness" (v. 2). His attributes and deeds are praiseworthy and always in view in the worship of the people of God. Lastly, we learn *how* we are to praise him: "Praise him with trumpet sound…lute and harp…tambourine and dance…strings and pipe…sounding cymbals…loud clashing cymbals" (vv. 3-5).

The whom, where, and why of praising God is captured in other parts of our discussion, but the last point, *how* we are to praise him, is an aspect of the Psalms that demands special attention. We will look next at several categories of *how* we should praise the Lord.

PRAISE HIM WITH OUR HEARTS

It is fitting that we begin with the heart of praise. The Psalms present a vivid picture of the heart within us exploding into praise outside of us:

I give thanks to you, O Lord my God,
with my whole heart,
and I will glorify your name forever. (86:12)

Praise the LORD!
I will give thanks to the LORD
with my whole heart,
in the company of the upright,
in the congregation. (111:1)

The emphasis on praising the Lord with "my whole heart" (e.g., 86:12) reminds us that the worship of God should have a consuming quality. It should fill our minds and emotions to such an extent that we cannot help but respond outwardly. Further, such exhortations forbid all kinds of "going through the motions" or hypocrisy. Hypocrisy is expressing things outwardly we do not at all feel inwardly. Hypocrisy is when we lift our hands and our voices to sing God's praises, but inwardly feel nothing at all toward him and want only to cast off his commands and lordship. If this happens here and there, we can accept it as part of the human condition—fallen and in need of glorification. If this happens routinely, maybe we need to pull away and sort out the angst in our souls. Let our praise begin in our hearts and then overflow into these other expressions of praise.

PRAISE HIM WITH OUR VOICES

Next we look at the variety of ways that we are commanded to praise God with our voices. This is the most natural form of praise there is, and it is also the least controversial. Saints from all traditions and generations have a history of praising God with their voices. Whether someone is Charismatic or Calvinistic, Methodist or Mennonite, this is a part of their Sunday gatherings. The Psalms are filled with commands along these lines:

> *Sing praises to the LORD,*
> *who sits enthroned in Zion!*
> *Tell among the peoples his deeds! (9:11)*
>
> *Sing praises to God, sing praises!*
> *Sing praises to our King, sing praises!*
> *For God is the King of all the earth;*
> *sing praises with a psalm! (47:6-7)*
>
> *I will extol you, my God and King,*
> *and bless your name forever and ever. (145:1)*

These excerpts capture only part of the variety of the Psalms. The Psalms are filled with loud and declarative expressions: *shout, extol, declare, exult* (33:1; 30:1; 145:4; 9:2). We see the musical displays: *sing aloud, sing praises, sing a new song, sing for joy* (33:1-3; 96:1-2; etc.). We see the plainer displays: *bless, speak, speak the praise* (103:1-2; 145:21). All of these are the overflow of a heart enthralled by the glorious God they behold by faith. Some of these are spontaneous outbursts: *shout for joy, sing to the LORD a new song* (66:1-2). Others seem more thoughtful and intentional: *speak of the might of your awesome deeds, declare your greatness* (145:6). In almost every Psalm we find some way to praise the Lord with our voices.

PRAISE HIM WITH OUR BODIES

Praising the Lord includes singing and speech, but it involves our bodies just as surely as cheering on our favorite football team causes us to raise our hands at the last-second touchdown. Thus, with our bodies we bow, dance, clap our hands, and lift our hands:

> *I bow down toward your holy temple*
> *and give thanks to your name*
> *for your steadfast love and your faithfulness. (138:2)*
>
> *You have turned for me*
> *my mourning into dancing. (30:11*
>
> *Clap your hands, all peoples. (47:1)*
>
> *Lift up your hands to the holy place. (134:2)*

These expressions are not exhaustive, but suggestive. They paint a picture of a worshiper enthralled with the glory of God and the redemption the Lord has accomplished. While such physical displays demand thoughtful consideration as we bring them into corporate worship, let us at the very least acknowledge that they are thoroughly biblical.

PRAISE HIM WITH OUR INSTRUMENTS

As a guitar player for twenty-six years with a degree in music, this next dimension of our praise is a particular favorite. Along with our heart and our voice we are to praise God with instruments. In fact, we are commanded to do so. Instruments were not a part of the worship of Israel in a formal way until King David developed a tradition of Levitical worshipers. In 1 Chronicles 25 we are in the middle of many chapters of David's organization of the people of God. Part of this includes provision for temple musicians. We read of those "who prophesied with lyres and harps and with cymbals" and those "who prophesied with the lyre in thanksgiving and praise to the LORD" (25:3). Others "were trained in singing to the LORD" (v. 7). Forever after this the praises of God even in the temple itself included a variety of instruments. This instrumental praise finds expression throughout the Psalms:

Give thanks to the LORD with the lyre;
Make melody to him
with the harp of ten strings!...
Play skillfully on the strings, with loud shouts. (33:2,3)

I will sing a new song to you, O God;
upon a ten-stringed harp I will play to you. (144:9)

Make melody to our God on the lyre. (147:7)

Let them praise his name with dancing,
making melody to him
with tambourine and lyre. (149:3)

Praise him with trumpet sound;
Praise him with lute and harp! (150:3)

Praise him with sounding cymbals;
Praise him with loud clashing cymbals! (150:5)

Again we find a great variety. It might be the private musician on his "ten-stringed lyre" (144:9) or the "loud clashing cymbals" (150:5) of the gathered orchestra of praise. "Trumpet sound" certainly communicates something different than "lute and harp" (150:3), and yet both are engaged in praising God. Thus, by explicit mention we have strings, horns, and percussion added to the choirs of the last section. These references are merely pointers, however. We are not to slavishly try and capture these archaic instruments in our services. These are better seen as pointers and indicators that our praises should involve the instruments—many of them!—of our day for this highest of purposes. Discernment will need to be exercised to sort out what will be most edifying to the church we have. It is easy to see that the small country church's piano works just fine, but the urban church might need more dynamism to encourage their people in praise.

PRAISE HIM WITH OTHERS

We also need to see within the praises in the Psalms their corporate dimension. Worship has a private side, but there must also be occasions where we gather as the people of God to praise him. Throughout the Psalms we have exhortations to the gathered people of God to lift up his name:

We give thanks to you, O God;
we give thanks, for your name is near.
We recount your wondrous deeds. (75:1)

Sing aloud to God our strength;
shout for joy to the God of Jacob. (81:1, all the verbs are plural)

Oh come, let us sing to the LORD;
let us make a joyful noise
to the rock of our salvation! (95:1)

We could add to the above references the word *hallelujah*, the call to "Praise the LORD" found in Psalms 146-150. This imperative is a plural one and could be translated, "All of you praise the LORD!"

Thus, throughout the Psalter we have occasions when the saints of God praise him ("we give thanks," 75:1), but also calls to the earth itself (97:1), and for all heavenly and earthly beings to join in praising God (148:2, 11). Our Sunday services capture an aspect of this, but these are also only a sampling of the raucous praise that is to be lifted up by all creation and all creatures. The apostle John sees just such a worship service in heaven itself (Rev. 5:11-14).

PRAISE HIM ALONE

Our praise is also to have a solitary side. Much of our life is lived away from the saints of God, but that does not mean the praise should end. The psalmists of the Bible were given to the praise of God whether they were gathered with other believers or in the starkest isolation:

My mouth is filled with your praise,
and with your glory all the day. (71:8)

I will extol you, my God and King,
and bless your name forever and ever.
Every day I will bless you
and praise your name forever and ever. (145:1-2)

I will sing a new song to you. (144:9)

I will praise the LORD as long as I live;
I will sing praises to my God
while I have my being. (146:2)

As individual followers of Christ we are to "extol" and "bless" and "praise" him even when we are alone. In fact, we should even "sing a new song" when we have occasion. It may not be a good song or a song others should hear, but the fact it comes from a sincere heart of praise will make it a sweet song in the ears of God.

The call to do this "every day" challenges us as well. In seasons of joy and triumph or hardship and darkness, let us be those who praise him. Without a doubt it is easier to read about

Job's worship in the midst of his distress (Job 1:20-22) than it is to do it. God help us to be a people of praise in all seasons of our lives.

We could say much more from the Psalter about praise, but these passages help us see what a people of praise looks like. They praise him out of their hearts, with their voices, with their bodies, with instruments, with others, and alone. Such praise does not end with the coming of Christ. Christ is now our tabernacle and fulfills all that the tabernacle points to, but the praises lifted up within the tabernacle and temple continue. God's people are *always* to be a people of praise.

PRAISE IN THE NEW TESTAMENT

As we move toward the New Testament we learn that the great difference is not *whether* or not we should praise the Lord or *how* we should praise him, but it is *why* we praise him. The content of our praises now includes the work of redemption that he accomplished in Jesus Christ. The New Testament abounds in examples of this.

We read of a "multitude of the heavenly host praising God" at the announcement of the birth of Jesus (Luke 2:13; cf. 2:20). The apostle Paul speaks of our salvation as being "to the praise[iii] of his glorious grace" and "to the praise of his glory" (vv. 6, 12, 14). He also says that our sanctification will be "to the glory and praise of God" (Phil. 1:11). Additionally, in Romans we learn that part of the work of Christ is seen in the Gentiles "praising"[iv] the Lord (Rom. 15:11). Sometimes God is praised as people experience the blessings of Christ, as when the paralytic is healed in the temple and is seen "walking and leaping and praising God" (Acts 3:8-9).

The musical aspects of praise do not receive much attention in the New Testament, but in Colossians and Ephesians we have the exhortations to "sing psalms and hymns and spiritual songs" (Eph. 5:19; Col. 3:16; cf. 1 Cor. 14:26). Further, the mention of "harps" as the heavenly saints praise the Lord suggests that instruments always retain a place in corporate worship (5:8; 14:2; 15:2).

Revelation reminds us that praises do not diminish at the consummation, but they actually increase. In chapter five we read that the "four living creatures and the twenty-four elders"

sang a new song, saying,
"Worthy are you to take the scroll
and to open its seals,
for you were slain,
and by your blood
you ransomed people for God
from every tribe and language
and people and nation,
10 *and you have made them*
a kingdom and priests to our God,
and they shall reign on the earth." (Rev. 5:9-10)

Thus, as we consider the praises of God throughout the Bible, how right is the command of Hebrews 13:15: "Through him then let us continually offer up a sacrifice of praise to God, that is, the fruit of lips that acknowledge his name."

SUNDAY AND EVERYDAY

Worship means proclaiming—either implicitly or explicitly—the glory of God. We do this through our obedience, sacrifice, and praise. This means that worship should touch every nanosecond and square inch of our lives. Driving our car to work can be worship as we sing his praises in the car. Taking care of our finances can be worship as we connect this to our obedience to God. Loving our children and spouse can be worship as we sacrifice on their behalf with an awareness that this is also done for Christ. And of course Sunday mornings become the great high point of our week as we gather with all the saints to sing his praises and exalt his name in all the ways that the Bible instructs us. And all of this is a mere foretaste of the worship that will erupt out of our souls and mouths and bodies in the new heavens and new earth where we see him as he truly is.

Before we complete this section on foundational truths in our worship, we need to consider one more area of vital importance, namely, how our worship connects to the Lord Jesus Christ.

NOTES

[i] From the most common Hebrew root for "praise," the piel of *halal*.

[ii] For more reflection on the Psalms see the appendix.

[iii] Greek, *epainon.*

[iv] From the Greek *exomologeō.*

CHAPTER THREE

Jesus Christ: the Center of it All

OUR CONTINENTAL DIVIDE

In Glacier National Park there is a mountain called Triple Divide Peak. Its height is respectable at over 8,000 feet, but it is something else that gives it such fame. It gets its name because two continental divides converge at its summit. That means that depending on where the rain and snow fall on its peak, water can travel hundreds of miles to the Pacific (via the Flathead and Columbia Rivers), thousands of miles to the Gulf of Mexico (ultimately through the Mississippi River), or thousands of miles to the Atlantic Ocean (via the Hudson Bay). Scientists call it a "hydrological apex." How water lands with respect to the summit makes all the difference for its final destination.[1]

The apex that makes all the difference for us is Jesus Christ. There is no way we can worship rightly without thinking rightly about and responding rightly to Jesus. If we get confused about who he is and what he taught about worship we will never get clarity about our worship. Good intentions and sincere emotions are not enough to please God with our worship. We must also wrestle with what he has revealed to us in the Scriptures. And central to what he has revealed is his Son Jesus Christ.

While we could write volumes on this topic we will focus on three things: what Jesus taught, what Jesus accomplished, and who Jesus is.

WHAT JESUS TAUGHT

Jesus taught a great deal about worship throughout his ministry, but one passage seems particularly helpful as a starting point for this chapter, John 4. It is here that we find the most extensive teaching by Jesus on our subject. In this chapter Jesus is traveling from the Jordan River to Galilee, and he passes through Samaria. While resting and waiting for the disciples, a "woman from Samaria" (v. 7) comes to the well where he is. During the conversation that ensues the woman makes a comment about her fathers who "worshiped on this mountain, but you say that in Jerusalem is the place where people ought to worship" (v. 20). In other words, it is a statement about *where* true worship can be offered. Jesus answers with the following:

> *Jesus said to her, "Woman, believe me, the hour is coming when neither on this mountain nor in Jerusalem will you worship the Father. [22] You worship what you do not know; we worship what we know, for salvation is from the Jews. [23] But the hour is coming, and is now here, when the true worshipers will worship the Father in spirit and truth, for the Father is seeking such people to worship him. [24] God is spirit, and those who worship him must worship in spirit and truth." (John 4:21-24)*

Jesus makes three points here germane to our topic. The first is that the *place* of worship is about to change. Since Moses, true worship has always been centered in a particular place, namely, the tabernacle (then the temple of Solomon). This was the place where sacrifices were offered, the priests would minister, and the people would gather. But Jesus is telling us here that worship will soon be completely disconnected from such a fixed location. Despite the numerous references in the Old Testament and the intensity of Jewish expectations, true worship would now have nothing to do with a mountain in Samaria (it never did) or a temple in Jerusalem. We can see the smallest trace of this idea if we imagine being in a school library in the 80s and thumbing through our Encyclopedia Britannica. Then someone comes up and begins to describe Wikipedia to us. We would have no idea what they were talking about. "What? Knowledge that is simply traveling through the air to my screen, available anywhere, anytime? You're talking science fiction." But indeed, true worship will now be offered anywhere God's people are truly worshiping him, whether it is in a school gym, a coffee shop, a living room, or a gorgeously ornate church building.

Jesus' second point is about our worship being *biblical.* Just because we prefer worship a certain way does not make it right. There really is a wrong way to worship God. Jesus clarifies this by telling the woman that she is actually worshiping "what you do not know" (v. 22). He is saying that her worship is based on false teachings and false understandings so distorted that they do not truly "know" what or whom they are even worshiping. The problem is that the Samaritans abandoned the teaching of Moses and developed their own way of worshiping their own image of the Lord (1 Ki. 12:25ff.). Their worship was thus false worship from the very beginning. Why? Because it was not according to the word of the Lord that he had given to his people. True worship must be according to the word of the Lord as it has been given to us.

Jesus' third point is about what *true* worship is. He says that "the true worshipers will worship the Father in spirit and truth....God is spirit, and those who worship must worship in spirit and truth" (vv. 23, 24). True worship has these two components to it, though they are inseparable. It is "in spirit" and it is "in truth."

To worship "in spirit" means to worship "in the Holy Spirit."[ii] This idea has several sides to it that come together in our worship. We are "born of the Spirit" (John 3:5-8) when we are "born again" (v. 7). At that moment we go from being dead in our flesh to alive in the Spirit. We go from being powerless to defeat temptation to being filled with the grace of God. To "worship in spirit" means that we must be spiritually reborn before we can offer true worship.

It also describes the kind of fellowship we have with God. The God who "is Spirit" can only be accessed spiritually. One day we shall see him and touch him, but now we walk by faith and fellowship with him through the Holy Spirit. In worship we experience this fellowship.

Worshiping "in spirit" also points to the spiritual gifts of the post-Pentecost church. This is the outworking of God's Spirit within us that flows out of us "like rivers of living water" (John 7:38). Paul will develop this idea much more fully as we will see (1 Cor. 12-14), but the idea is presented here in seed form.[iii]

To worship "in truth" means a couple different things as well. We know that Jesus *is* "the truth" and not simply one who teaches true things (John 14:6). So to worship "in truth" means that we are worshiping in Christ. It is to be in him, to be born again in him, to be united to him, to live in him. If we are not connected to Jesus by faith we can never worship him "in truth."

But here we are also drawn to Jesus' teaching, the one who is "the Word" and brought "grace and truth" (John 1:1-4, 17). We cannot worship rightly if we do not listen to the words of Jesus. We must understand his teaching if our private and corporate worship is to be pleasing to him. This is what it means to worship "in truth." Thus, he taught the revelation of God because he *was* the revelation of God. He taught the truth of God because he *was* the truth of God.

So in this one passage from his teaching Jesus has said a great deal about our worship. We can summarize it in these six statements:

(1) True worship is not located in a specific location, but can be offered anywhere.
(2) True worship is rooted in the Word of God.
(3) True worship can only happen when we are born again.
(4) True worship will mean spiritual fellowship with God.
(5) True worship will involve spiritual gifts.

(6) True worship can only be given when we are in Christ.

Jesus will confirm these truths throughout his teaching, but this passage has given us a good introduction to what Jesus taught about worship. Now we turn to how the cross of Christ impacts our worship.

WHAT JESUS ACCOMPLISHED

The cross of Christ affects worship profoundly. In fact, apart from the cross there would be no worship. Apart from Christ, we are a mass of idolaters and sinners with no hope of becoming a people of God who proclaim the God's surpassing glory. In this section we will thus unpack a few of the key ways that *what Jesus accomplished* impacts our worship.

First, Jesus's redemption makes worshippers out of idolaters. Romans 1:25 vividly describes what we were like before we were converted. There we are described as those who "exchanged the truth about God for a lie and worshiped and served the creature rather than the Creator, who is blessed forever!" We were certainly worshipers before we were Christians, but we were worshiping "the creature rather than the Creator." It was the stuff of this world that dominated our hearts and souls and minds. The Creator was a distant (or even wretched) thought we worked to suppress.

The marvel of the cross is that we were not left in this condemnable state. God could have abandoned us and righteously poured out his wrath upon us for being such idolaters. Instead he sent his Son to save us. In Ephesians 1 we read that "in him we have redemption through his blood, the forgiveness of our trespasses" (v. 7). The idolatry that was ours has been forgiven through the "redemption" that Christ paid with "his blood." What is the result? In three places in Ephesians 1 Paul spells out that worship is the result: "he predestined us…to the praise of his glorious grace" (1:5, 6); "we have obtained an inheritance…to the praise of his glory" (1:11, 12); "you also…were sealed with the promised Holy Spirit…to the praise of his glory" (1:13, 14).

Do you see that? Idolaters like us who were given to worshiping the stuff of this world have been redeemed through the blood of Christ and worship is the result. The cross redeems idolaters who worship the creation and makes them believers who praise God's grace.

Second, Jesus's redemption removes all barriers to the very presence of God. The cross also radically fulfills the whole tabernacle system of worship. Part of that elaborate system was a division between the holy of holies and the outer courts. Anyone could enter the outer courts, but the holy of holies was restricted to the high priest and only once per year. The sobering fact of that division is that the manifest presence of God was inside the holy of holies. The cross changes all that. The author of Hebrews shows us that this greater and more perfect offering of Jesus did what the blood of animals could never do. When Christ offered "his own blood" (9:12), he "perfected for all time those who are being sanctified" (10:14) and he thus remembers our sins no more (10:17).

What is the result of such a redemption? It means that we can "have confidence to enter the holy places by the blood of Jesus, by the new and living way that he opened for us through the curtain, that is, through his flesh" (10:19-20). The separation is gone—remember that the curtain in the temple was torn "from top to bottom" when Jesus died (Matt. 27:51).

So, our worship is not offered from a distance, from an outer court separated from the presence of God. Now we can confidently enter the very presence of God! In fact, we *are already* in the presence of God. In worship we are not going from outside the presence of God to inside his presence (as was true of the high priest on the Day of Atonement, Lev. 16). We are moving into a greater awareness of his presence or experience of his presence. He is present in a special way when his people gather to worship, but we should not confuse that with what Jesus accomplished on the cross. When I am alone in my living room all barriers to the presence of God have been removed, and if I am a Christian then I can enjoy his presence even there (Heb. 10:19-25). But I am still eager to worship God corporately among his people, because there he is present in an even greater way.

Third, Jesus inaugurates a new covenant, which means a new experience of God and a new way of reading the Old Testament. A third way that what Jesus accomplished impacts our worship is by inaugurating a new covenant. The Bible often speaks of covenants, and we can think of these as an agreement that God makes with us where he promises to do certain things on our behalf, and in some of these covenants he demands certain things of us. In the Old Testament one of the most important of these covenants is the one made at Mt. Sinai through Moses. This is where Israel was given the Law, which included the Ten Commandments (Ex. 19-24). At Mt. Sinai, Moses sprinkled blood on the people and on the Ten Commandments to symbolize the formation of this covenant (Ex. 24:8). Centuries later God promised that he would "make a new covenant with the house of Israel and the house of Judah," a covenant unlike all previous covenants in the Bible (Jer. 31:31-34).

All of this is the backdrop of Jesus' words at the last supper when Jesus says, "This cup that is poured out for you is the new covenant in my blood" (Luke 22:20). He is telling us here that the covenant promised in Jeremiah 31 would now be inaugurated by the shedding of his blood, just like blood was shed at Mt. Sinai when the old covenant was inaugurated. In other words: no Jesus, no new covenant; no cross, no new covenant.

Here is the prophecy regarding the new covenant:

> *"Behold, the days are coming, declares the LORD, when I will make a new covenant with the house of Israel and the house of Judah,*
> *32 not like the covenant that I made with their fathers on the day when I took them by the hand to bring them out of the land of Egypt, my covenant that they broke, though I was their husband, declares the LORD.*
> *33 But this is the covenant that I will make with the house of Israel after those days, declares the LORD: I will put my law within them, and I will write it on their hearts. And I will be their God, and they shall be my people.*
> *34 And no longer shall each one teach his neighbor and each*

> *his brother, saying, 'Know the LORD,' for they shall all know me, from the least of them to the greatest, declares the LORD. For I will forgive their iniquity, and I will remember their sin no more." (Jer. 31:31-34)*

Right in the middle of this excerpt, God says he will "put my law within them" and "write it on their hearts" (v. 33). Now the ability to do the will of God will be inside of us through the Holy Spirit. Further, "they shall all know me." Knowledge of God will not be the exclusive possession of prophets, priests, and kings, but everyone will have equal access to God. Last, "I will forgive their iniquity," not in the partial way of animal sacrifices, but in the perfect and forever complete way of the offering of Jesus Christ (Heb. 10:18). All of this is accomplished because of the cross of Christ.

The cross also forever changes our worship. Now we no longer go to the temple, wait on the priests, and approach God through various sacrifices. Instead we "draw near to the throne of grace, that we may receive mercy and find grace to help in time of need" (Heb. 4:16). Life in the new covenant means more ability to know and do the will of God through the Holy Spirit, more knowledge of God, and complete forgiveness of sins. Freedom, power, and peace: That's what it means to experience the new covenant. All of this is ours in Christ through his cross.

Of course, the fact that we live under a new covenant does not mean that everything spoken of in the Old Testament is not for us but merely for the Jews. Not only does the Old Testament give history and theology critical to understand God, ourselves, and the New Testament, but the New Testament makes it very clear that many commands in the Old Testament must still be obeyed. The author of Hebrews, for instance, quotes Psalm 95:7 and he calls this "the Holy Spirit speaking" (Heb. 3:7). Not just that the Holy Spirit *said*, but the Holy Spirit is saying to us right now, "Today if you hear his voice, do not harden your hearts." This is a command to be obeyed by God's people.

This means that our worship must listen to the Old Testament teaching to be thoroughly biblical. Not only does the

Old Testament reveal the God we worship and much about us the worshipers, but throughout it we learn what God wants us to do in our worship. He still wants us to "shout for joy" and "sing the glory of his name" and "give to him glorious praise" (Ps. 66:1-2). So let us be wise as we navigate through the Old Testament so that we do not adopt worship practices done away with by the cross of Christ, but let us make sure that we adopt those worship practices consistent with the gospel of Christ.[iv]

WHO JESUS IS

So Jesus radically changes our worship through his teaching and his redemption. Jesus also changes our worship because of *who he is*. Who Jesus is actually changes who we are to worship in the sense that our understanding of who we worship is expanded and deepened and broadened. No longer is it enough to cry along with the Jews the great Shemah: "Hear, O Israel: The LORD our God, the LORD is one. You shall love the LORD your God with all your heart" (Deut. 6:4-5). Our worship must include Jesus, the one Thomas rightfully called, "My Lord and my God!" (John 20:28).

This point is familiar and obvious to Christians, but it is helpful to remember this was indeed a dramatic change that Jesus brought to our worship. For the 1,500 years under the Law of Moses, worship was to be exclusively directed to the true God who had revealed himself as Yahweh—"I AM WHO I AM," the LORD who made all things, rescued them from Egypt, and was calling them to live the life prescribed in the Law. That he was Father, Son, and Spirit was hinted at, but never made clear and never expressed in their worship except in type and shadow.

With Jesus everything changed. Suddenly people who encountered his glory, especially through his miracles, would instinctively worship him. The man born blind and healed by Jesus professes, "Lord, I believe," and then "he worshiped him" (John 9:38). Jesus does something truly amazing at that point: he let him. He doesn't rebuke the man for being an idolater or for giving him the worship only due to God in heaven. He doesn't say that such actions are only worthy of a deity and that the man should therefore stand up. No, he let him because he indeed was the true and living God revealed in Jesus Christ. Just as the Jews worshiped Yahweh, so we are to give that same worship to Jesus. In fact, Jesus reveals that when the Jews worshiped Yahweh, they were actually worshiping him (John 8:58). We are simply to do so explicitly.

Our worship is thus to be thoroughly Trinitarian. We worship God as Father, Son, and Holy Spirit, and our worship should unmistakably capture this. In this way we are to imitate what we find in the book of Revelation where God and the Lamb are worshiped alongside one another: "To him who sits on the throne and to the Lamb be blessing and honor and glory and might forever and ever!" (5:13). Jesus changed our worship by making it abundantly clear that we are to worship *him*.

SUNDAY AND EVERY DAY

Jesus is clearly the 'hydrological apex' of our worship. He is the point that alters the course of everything he touches. This reminds us that our worship is to be distinctly *Christian* worship—worship that is defined by, given to, and happening only in Christ. There are several practical implications of this fact.

First, Sunday corporate worship is not a process of being far from the presence of God and needing to be led into his presence. The curtain has been torn, our sins have been paid for, and we have a true and real relationship with God. We cannot be any more in God's presence than we already are. No matter the sins we committed this week, or the total absence of devotions, or the many things we failed to do for Christ, we remain in God's presence. He does not disown us when we sin or even push us away, giving us some kind of cold shoulder. All judgment has been taken away by Christ—all of it! This means that we don't earn our confidence to draw near to him. Remember the words of Hebrews 10:19, "Therefore, brothers,...we have confidence to enter the holy places by the blood of Jesus." Who is it that does the work here? It is Jesus. Who is it that offers the sacrifice? It is Jesus. Our sins and weaknesses are not greater than "the blood of Jesus." Therefore, come with confidence in private and in corporate worship. The Father will welcome you with open arms!

Of course, what does ebb and flow is our awareness of his presence, our felt sense of his presence. Along these lines, God inhabits the corporate praise of his people in a uniquely intensive way. This should make us especially happy to gather with God's people in worship, because through his Spirit there is indeed a special blessing on these times. We will see more of God's special blessing on the corporate meeting in Part Two of our discussion. So, while God's presence is not uniquely exclusive to our corporate worship, it is uniquely intensive.

Second, the entire Bible should inform our worship. Jesus does not make our Old Testament irrelevant, he makes it understandable. Now we can turn to its pages and apply what we read there to our private and corporate worship. The key is to interpret our Old Testament through the lens of the teaching of the New Testament and all that we said about Jesus Christ. Once we have done that, however, the Psalms, the books of Moses, the prophets, and all else in the Old Testament should speak to our worship.

How much more there is to say about the place of Jesus in our worship, but hopefully these two ideas give us a starting point.

****

We have now laid the foundation for our understanding of worship. It is to proclaim his unrivalled glory, and we do this through our obedience, sacrifice, and praise. And all of this is done with Jesus Christ at the center of it all. These understandings provide the foundation and framework for everything that follows. But because worship must actually be expressed corporately as the people of God, we have much more ground to cover before we have a complete picture of what biblical worship is. That is where we go next.

NOTES

[i] Obtained from http://www.nps.gov/glac/forteachers/continental_divide.htm on April 11, 2011.

[ii] There are two basic views on this. Either Jesus means our human spirit or the Holy Spirit. Because of the way John typically uses "spirit" (*pneuma*), I am persuaded that it refers to the Holy Spirit (e.g., 1:32-33; 3:5-8; 14:17, 26; 15:26; 16:13; 1 John 4:1-13; etc.). At times he refers to the human "spirit" (John 13:17; 19:30), but in those places it is explicit

what he means. Those affirming that it means our human spirit include Leon Morris, *The Gospel According to John,* NICNT (Grand Rapids, MI: William B. Eerdmans Publishing Co., 1995); John Piper, *Desiring God* (Colorado Springs, CO: Multnomah Books, 2011*);* and Skip Ryan, *That You May Believe: New Life in the Son* (Wheaton, IL: Crossway Books, 2003*)*. Those affirming that the Holy Spirit is referenced include Herman Ridderbos, *The Gospel of John: A Theological Commentary* (Grand Rapids, MI: William B. Eerdmans Publishing, Co., 1997; D.A. Carson, *The Gospel According to John,* PNTC (Grand Rapids, MI: William B. Eerdmans Publishing, Co., 1990); and Bruce Milne, *The Message of John,* Bible Speaks Today (Leicester, England: InterVarsity Press, 1993).

[iii] See chapter five on spiritual gifts for more development of this issue.

[iv] These ideas are represented in Reformed theology by the notion that the Old Testament contains three types of law: (1) moral, (2) ceremonial, and (3) civil. *The Westminster Confession of Faith* is one expression of this, though by no means is it the only one. Chapter 19 speaks extensively to the three types of law, and it says that "the law" given to Adam was a moral law to be obeyed (19:1). It was "a perfect rule of righteousness" and was further elaborated on at Mount Sinai in the "ten commandments" (19:2). Added to this moral law were the "ceremonial laws" that contained types that anticipated Christ (19:3). Mostly these centered on the worship and sacrifice of the Levitical priestly system, but there were other laws as well. All of these laws "are now abrogated under the new testament" (ibid.). The third type of law is sometimes called the "civil law," but in the Westminster Confession they are called "sundry judicial laws," and these "expired together with the state of that people, not obliging any other now, further than the general equity therefore may require" (19:4). The moral law continues and is even strengthened in the New Testament (19:5). Those laws that continue to be binding for the Christian are not "a covenant of works" that can save us, but they are "a rule of life, informing them of the will of God and their duty" (19:6). For a thorough and excellent treatment of this subject, see *From the Finger of God: The Biblical and Theological Basis for the Threefold Division of the Law* by Philip S. Ross (Mentor Books, 2011). For a more basic but still excellent introduction to these ideas, see Sinclair Ferguson's book *Sermon on the Mount* (Banner of Truth, 1988). One place where I diverge from Reformed theology is on making the moral law equivalent to the Ten Commandments. Because of places like Matthew 22:36ff.; Romans 12:9-21; Ephesians 4:25-32; and 1 Peter 1:16, etc., it is clear to me that the moral law as the apostles read it went far beyond the Ten Commandments. So while the Ten Commandments give

us one of the most important expressions of the moral law and certainly one of the most memorable, I believe that the moral law is any law that isn't tied to the ceremonial or civil life of Israel and which continues to be binding for Christians.

PART TWO

Corporate Worship

CHAPTER FOUR

The Components of Corporate Worship

NEGOTIABLES AND NON-NEGOTIABLES

What does a typical Sunday look like at your church? Do you sing or pray or read Scripture? Do you take up an offering? Do you listen to sermons or allow time for spiritual gifts? Do you ever show videos or do drama? But have you ever stopped and considered whether God wants you to do these things or not? Most of us haven't. Or at least not recently. We will plan this Sunday in a particular way pretty much because that's what we did last Sunday. And the Sunday before that. And the decade before that. But again, *Does God actually want you to do that?*

This chapter is a chance to stop and think about the different parts of our corporate worship. The heart of the discussion will be a list of what are the key biblical elements that our services should include, regularly if not every time.

Our church is by no means the first to wrestle with these issues. In fact, hundreds of years ago the Westminster divines (i.e., smart, religious guys in the 17th century) gave us two principles that can point us in the right direction. In the Westminster Confession of Faith they said first and most importantly that our worship is

> *instituted by [God], and so limited by His own revealed will, that He may not be worshipped according to the imaginations and devices of men, or the suggestions of Satan, under any visible representation, or any other way not prescribed in the Holy Scripture (21:1).*

This is the essence of what is called the "Regulative Principle," the idea that we worship only in ways specifically commanded in Scripture. This provides the "non-negotiables" of our corporate worship.

Yet, this is to be matched to a second idea found earlier in the Confession:

> *There are some circumstances concerning the worship of God, and government of the Church, common to human actions and societies, which are to be ordered by the light of nature, and Christian prudence, according to the general rules of the word, which are always to be observed (1:6).*

"Christian prudence" helps us with the "negotiables" of our corporate gatherings, the details that the Bible does not discuss.

Taking these two together, then, we order our worship firmly rooted to the Bible itself—its commands and examples and precedents. We start here and ruthlessly work to remain here. Even with this beginning, however, we will need to add a healthy dose of wisdom and common sense. The Bible might command us to sing, but it provides no melodies for us. It commands us to preach the word, but it provides no sermon outlines and no specifics about sermon length. We get various commands about the corporate meeting, but we are never told which ones are to be in every gathering, and which we can have only occasionally. This is where our "Christian prudence" is added to what is "prescribed in Holy Scripture."

In what follows we will work through the "non-negotiables" of our worship and then provide a few thoughts on how we think about the "negotiables."

WHAT THE BIBLE COMMANDS

Most books on worship contain a list of the components of our corporate worship (sometimes called the "elements of worship").[i] These lists are summaries of what the Bible commands in our corporate gatherings. Yet, as common as such lists are, no two lists are ever identical. This has to do with the person's worship tradition and with their interpretive approach to the Bible.

Generally, the places of agreement between evangelical authors are those practices that have clear Scriptural warrant. The differences between authors are areas where they are deriving practices from the Scriptures (e.g., benedictions which are modeled in the epistles, but not commanded of the gathered church). Further, our overall biblical and theological framework has a profound impact on what we see as normative practice for the gathered church of Jesus Christ. As an obvious example, many do not feel the need to include prophecy in their gatherings (cf. 1 Cor. 14:1ff.).

For our list, we will keep to what is clearly modeled or commanded in Scripture. This does not mean other elements should not or cannot be added (e.g., "calls to worship"), but that these will be secondary compared to what is of primary importance in our corporate worship. In essence, then, what we have here is the "bread and butter" of our worship. If we occasionally sprinkle in elements such as drama or practicalities such as announcements, that is not a problem. The only caveat is that these must serve the primary elements below and not the reverse. Further, this is the exhaustive list of those elements. It would not be practical therefore to include all of these in every service, but we should work to practice them regularly in our life together.

READING, PREACHING, AND TEACHING THE BIBLE

(DEUT. 31:10-12; NEH. 8; 1 TIM. 4:11, 13; 2 TIM. 4:1-2; JAMES 1:22-25)

Without a doubt, a primary part (*the* primary part) of our worship *must be* the reading, preaching, and teaching of Scripture. One of the tragic developments in our day is a drift away from connecting corporate worship to the routine exposition of the Bible. This was one of the foundational convictions of the Reformation, has served the church for centuries, and it has always been central to God's church whenever it is thriving and growing. When God's people lose their grip on his word, the vitality of his church slowly ebbs away, like a small leak in a car tire. On a given day the change might be imperceptible, but over time it means the difference between life and death, growing and languishing.

For many of us this point will seem obvious, but we should never let its familiarity dull us to its power and radical implications. God's people need God's word because they need God. His word is the *only fully reliable* source of truth about God, humanity, and creation. Thus, the Word of God must have a preeminent place in our local church:

> *And they devoted themselves to the apostles' teaching. (Acts 2:42)*
>
> *Command and teach these things....Until I come, devote yourself to the public reading of Scripture, to exhortation, to teaching. (1 Tim. 4:11, 13)*
>
> *I charge you in the presence of God and of Christ Jesus, who is to judge the living and the dead, and by his appearing and his kingdom: [2] preach the word; be ready in season and out of season; reprove, rebuke, and exhort, with complete patience and teaching. (2 Tim. 4:1-2)*

This is why a chief requirement for elders is that they be "able to teach" (1 Tim. 3:2).

God help us to preserve the place of the Scriptures in our corporate worship. Let us never grow weary of having them read, taught, sung, prayed, believed, and obeyed. Nothing will serve the next generation of the church more than working to give the Scriptures their proper place in our meetings and gatherings.

PRAYER
(ACTS 2:42; 1 TIM. 2:1-2, 8)

A second foundational activity for the gathered people of God is prayer. Where the Scriptures are God speaking to us, prayer is primarily us speaking to God. It is the way that we cry for help, express our longings, and relate to the God with whom we have a true relationship. We can see prayer in the early church from its earliest moments:

> *And they devoted themselves to the apostles' teaching and the fellowship, to the breaking of bread and the prayers. (Acts 2:42)*

Further, what is modeled in that scene is commanded by the apostle Paul:

> *First of all, then, I urge that supplications, prayers, intercessions, and thanksgivings be made for all people, [2] for kings and all who are in high positions, that we may lead a peaceful and quiet life, godly and dignified in every way....I desire then that in every place the men should pray, lifting holy hands without anger or quarreling. (1 Tim. 2:1-2, 8)*

Paul gives us some sense of the variety of ways that we can pray. Our prayers will include "prayers, intercessions, and thanksgivings." We do this "for kings and all who are in high positions," and we do it for the basic needs that we face. After all, Jesus felt that even our "daily bread" is a focus of our prayers (Matt. 6:11). The New Testament reveals further that we pray "in tongues" (1 Cor. 14:1-39), and we "pray in the Spirit" (Eph. 6:18; Jude v. 20). We also pray for our sicknesses, express gratitude for God's blessings, and confess our sins (James 5:13-16). Finally, we pray for the glory of God to be accomplished “on earth as it is in heaven” (Matt. 6:9-10). All of this is approaching the throne of grace to "receive mercy and find grace to help in time of need" (Heb. 4:16).

There are many dangers that accompany public prayers in the gathered church, most of which turn our prayers into religious displays. At times we pray more for those who are hearing us pray than for the Lord to whom we are praying. Crafting our prayers is indeed a service to those who hear us and a recognition that praying publicly is different than praying privately. Yet, when that craftsmanship makes us forget the point of our prayers—a heart engaging with the true and living God—then we have lost our way.

Prayer is often an accurate barometer for our true sense of need. Those who feel their need for God pray; those who do not feel their need for him do not pray. What do our services communicate about our sense of need? Do they show that we realize that apart from God's immediate and continual intervention both our lives and our church will fall apart? Or do they communicate that we basically have it covered, but a little bit more from the Lord would be helpful? Let us see that in Jesus "all things hold together" (Col. 1:17) and apart from him "you can do nothing" (John 15:5), and let us pray accordingly.

SINGING AND MUSICAL ACCOMPANIMENT
(1 COR. 14:26; EPH. 5:18-21; COL. 3:16)

Much has already been made about praising God with our bodies, voices, and instruments. As we argued before, the New Testament nowhere teaches that the instrumental and vocal worship of the Old Testament is done away with. The worship of the church age and even in the new heavens and new earth reveals a strong connection to the picture revealed in the Psalms:

> *When you come together, each one has a hymn, a lesson, a revelation, a tongue, or an interpretation. Let all things be done for building up. (1 Cor. 14:26)*

> *And do not get drunk with wine, for that is debauchery, but be filled with the Spirit, [19] addressing one another in psalms and hymns and spiritual songs, singing and making melody to the Lord with your heart. (Eph. 5:18-19)*

> *And when he had taken the scroll, the four living creatures and the twenty-four elders fell down before the Lamb, each holding a harp, and golden bowls full of incense, which are the prayers of the saints. And they sang a new song. (Rev. 5:8-9)*

The use of singing and instruments takes great wisdom and care, but let us work toward the whole array of musical expressions that we find in the Old and New Testaments.

PROPHECY, TONGUES, AND SPIRITUAL GIFTS (1 COR. 12-14)

An additional set of worship practices is summarized well for us in 1 Corinthians 14:26-30:

> *What then, brothers? When you come together, each one has a hymn, a lesson, a revelation, a tongue, or an interpretation. Let all things be done for building up. [27] If any speak in a tongue, let there be only two or at most three, and each in turn, and let someone interpret. [28] But if there is no one to interpret, let each of them keep silent in church and speak to himself and to God. [29] Let two or three prophets speak, and let the others weigh what is said. [30] If a revelation is made to another sitting there, let the first be silent. (1 Cor. 14:26-30)*

Because of the complexity and controversy of this topic we will devote chapter five to unpacking this issue. Indeed, New Testament worship must include the practice and pursuit of spiritual gifts. Technically speaking, it is impossible to *exclude* these from our gatherings, for if the church contains Christians then it necessarily contains Christians gifted by the Spirit (Eph. 4:7; 1 Cor. 12:7; 1 Peter 4:10-11). Teaching and leadership are spiritual gifts, after all.

COLLECTING TITHES AND OFFERINGS FOR THE MINISTRY OF THE CHURCH, THE POOR, CHURCHES IN NEED, AND VARIOUS ASPECTS OF OUR LOCAL AND EXTRA-LOCAL MISSION

(LEV. 27:30; MAL. 3:10; ACTS 2:45; 4:34-35; 1 COR. 16:1-3; 2 COR. 8-9; GAL. 6:6; PHIL. 4:10-19; 1 TIM. 5:3-16; MATT. 28:18-20)

Another side of our worship is where our "offering of praise" becomes quite tangible. It has always been the case that part of being the people of God is giving our financial resources to the Lord. There are two sides of this giving, one being the worship dimension of the activity and the other being the practical impact this giving has.

The worship side of this is evident in Philippians 4:18:

> *I have received full payment, and more. I am well supplied, having received from Epaphroditus the gifts you sent, a fragrant offering, a sacrifice acceptable and pleasing to God. (Phil. 4:18)*

Their gift helped him financially, but the apostle connects their giving to the Lord himself by calling it "a sacrifice acceptable and pleasing to God."

The second side of our giving is the practical impact it has on the church both locally and extra-locally. Our giving provides for the local elders and ministry of the church, as is surely intended in Galatians 6:6, "One who is taught the word must share all good things with the one who teaches." Paul is more explicit in 1 Timothy 5:18, "The laborer deserves his wages."

Our giving affects the people of God locally also as it provides for those in need. The young church of Acts 2 demonstrates this beautifully: "And they were selling their possessions and belongings and distributing the proceeds to all, as any had need" (v. 45).

This giving extends extra-locally as well when we support ministers of the gospel in other regions and those in need outside of our immediate context. The Philippian gift to Paul is supporting ministry extra-locally. In our church this means supporting our denomination as it works extra-locally on our behalf.

Yet, we also give extra-locally as material needs become known to us and our hearts are stirred. The early church sent money to Jerusalem to help with the famine there and to provide for the poor in that city church (Acts 11:27-30). The Corinthians collected money to help "the churches of Galatia" (1 Cor. 16:1-3).

Our giving is thus worship and material provision for those in need. It sustains ministers of the gospel and also helps the poor with basic necessities. Because both testaments regard our giving in such consistent ways we see the Old Testament "tithe" (*one-tenth*) as a principle that extends into the new covenant church. The advent of Jesus Christ does not bring any great change or disruption into this practice, only a change in the details of the gift. Now we give to our local church instead of the Levitical priests and the temple.

While it is true that "each one must give as he has decided in his heart, not reluctantly or under compulsion, for God loves a cheerful giver" (2 Cor. 9:7), the tithe remains a benchmark for us to guide our giving. A tithe is possible for almost all of us, though in some situations even that is beyond our reach. Yet, the discipline of giving the tithe often helps us retain some priority and order in our finances. It is also a way to make the lordship of Christ tangible and meaningful.

The biblical picture, then, for our giving, is that *with cheerful, Christ-centered hearts we give at least the tithe to our local church and above this as we are able*. In a day like ours where materialism and consumerism bombard us at every turn, let us fight to remain faithful and generous givers to the Lord by giving to our church (and beyond as we can!).

THESE FIVE AND OUR WEEKLY GATHERING

For our church the Bible, prayer, singing, offerings, and spiritual gifts are a kind of core that mark all of our corporate gatherings (i.e., Sunday services). This has to do with their prominence in the

Bible and also the singular impact they have on the body of Christ. They "build up" in ways unique and profound. This is not to say that the other elements which follow do not also build up the body of Christ intensively, especially the Lord's Supper, but only that these first five provide an excellent framework in which to place the remaining ones.

THE LORD'S SUPPER AND BAPTISM

(1 COR. 11:17-30; MATT. 28:19-20)[ii]

Next to the Bible and prayer, the most prominent element of New Testament worship is the Lord's Supper. That might surprise many of us who worship in traditions with monthly or quarterly celebrations of the Lord's Supper. Yet, all three synoptics record the last supper of Jesus in great detail (Matt. 26:16-29; Mark 14:12-25; Luke 22:7-23), the apostle Paul gives a full-length description of the practice in 1 Corinthians 11:17-34, and in the book of Acts we read of several occasions when the practice was recorded (Acts 2:42; 20:7). Considering the scarcity of references to the worship of the early church, the repeated mention of the Lord's Supper becomes significant. We will devote chapter six to a full treatment of the subject.

The Lord's Supper is one of two "ordinances" in the church, the second being baptism. Jesus commanded the church to baptize in the Great Commission:

> *Go therefore and make disciples of all nations, baptizing them in the name of the Father and of the Son and of the Holy Spirit, [20] teaching them to observe all that I have commanded you. And behold, I am with you always, to the end of the age." (Matt. 28:19-20)*

We can see in this passage that baptism is not practiced on infants, but "disciples." The disciples that are made through the efforts of the church are to be baptized and taught "all that I have commanded you." Since a disciple is a follower of the teachings and example of Jesus himself, it is inconsistent with the New

Testament picture to baptize infants (though some might be regenerate as John the Baptist seems to have been in Luke 1:41).

Another place where we see a simple presentation of the elements of baptism is Acts 16:30ff. There the Philippian jailer asks Paul and Silas, "What must I do to be saved?" (v. 30). They reply, "Believe in the Lord Jesus, and you will be saved, you and your household" (v. 31). After he dresses the wounds of the apostles, "he was baptized at once, he and all his family" (v. 33). We know his family believed as well because "he rejoiced along with his entire household that he had believed in God" (v. 34). Those old enough to "rejoice" are those who are baptized.

Who, then, is to be baptized? Those who "believe in the Lord Jesus," which means acknowledging Jesus as our Lord and Savior. As Lord he is Master of our lives, and we commit to do all we can to obey him—recognizing that our obedience will be perfect only when we are glorified. To call him Savior is to see his sacrificial death and resurrection as a complete payment for our sins (Rom. 3:21-28). In fact, it is the only adequate payment for our sins. Without Christ's blood we can expect only unending judgment for our many sins.

The Bible does not command the church to include baptisms in its corporate worship, but doing so can be a great means of grace to the body of Christ. We are wonderfully edified when we hear again the good news of the gospel and see another believer incorporated into the family of God.

It requires much reflection, wisdom, and simple trial-and-error to effectively incorporate the Lord's Supper and baptism into the regular corporate worship of the church. Yet, the effort is both worthwhile because these elements are so edifying, and it's essential because they are clearly part of New Testament church life.

CONFESSIONS OF FAITH

(ROM. 10:9-10; 1 COR. 15:3-4; 1 TIM. 3:16)

It is common in traditional churches to include in the liturgy occasional creeds and confessions of faith. The Nicene Creed, the Apostles Creed, and various other creeds are sometimes recited weekly. In many contemporary churches, such readings are excluded for various reasons, some good and some not so good. Such creeds can be a powerful summary of Christian orthodoxy (their original intent), and yet, like all things, they can be said mindlessly and coldly.

The Bible does not give us a clear picture on the use of such confessions. Places like Romans 10:9-10 help us see that a deliberate confession with our mouth is a significant demonstration of faith:

> *If you confess with your mouth that Jesus is Lord and believe in your heart that God raised him from the dead, you will be saved. [10] For with the heart one believes and is justified, and with the mouth one confesses and is saved. (Rom. 10:9-10)*

Such open "confession" seems in view in a passage like 1 Timothy 6:12 where the apostle mentions Timothy's "good confession in the presence of many witnesses."

Further, Paul seems to use creed-like forms in his writing. Here are two places suggestive of an established creed:

> *For I delivered to you as of first importance what I also received: that Christ died for our sins in accordance with the Scriptures, [4] that he was buried, that he was raised on the third day in accordance with the Scriptures. (1 Cor. 15:3-4)*

> *Great indeed, we confess, is the mystery of godliness: He was manifested in the flesh, vindicated by the Spirit, seen by angels, proclaimed among the nations, believed on in the world, taken up in glory. (1 Tim. 3:16)*

Beyond these hints at early practices we have little to go on.

Creeds in church history came into use early as controversy swept throughout regions, and precision was needed to establish points of doctrine. Thus, the person of Christ as fully God and fully man became the subject of the Nicene Creed, a clear and simple Trinitarian orthodoxy is seen in the Apostles Creed, etc. Such creeds were not at all seen as equal in authority to the Bible, but rather summaries of the Bible's teaching, litmus tests to establish orthodoxy in a church or person. Seen in this light, there is no reason at all to forbid their use in worship services. The risks attached to creeds and confessions arise when we lose the ability to defend biblically what is taught in them, or when they take on an authority equal to or even greater than the Bible itself. With these dangers acknowledged, the church is free to incorporate historical or contemporary creeds.

ORDINATION OF CHURCH OFFICERS
(ACTS 6:1-7; 13:1-3; 1 TIM. 4:14; 2 TIM. 1:6)

Another dimension of our corporate worship, perhaps less common in our regular meetings, is the ordination of church officers. When the first set of deacons is ordained in Acts 6 we read that the church "set [the deacons] before the apostles, and they prayed and laid their hands on them" (Acts 6:6). This was a public ceremony that brought a culmination to the process of identifying qualified servants who would now be stepping into their area of responsibility. In this case, they are deacons that will oversee the feeding of Hellenist widows in the Jerusalem church (6:1-5). The service will inevitably be different in our context, but the act of laying hands and praying to commission an officer is one we want to see carried on in our settings.

Paul and Barnabas are commissioned in a similar manner in Antioch, but their apostolic work is even more directly an outgrowth of the corporate worship of the church:

> *Now there were in the church at Antioch prophets and teachers, Barnabas, Simeon who was called Niger, Lucius of Cyrene, Manaen a member of the court of Herod the tetrarch, and Saul. ²While they were worshiping the Lord and fasting, the Holy Spirit said, "Set apart for me Barnabas and Saul for the work to which I have called them." ³Then after fasting and praying they*

> *laid their hands on them and sent them off. (Acts 13:1-3)*

As the gathered church is "worshiping the Lord and fasting," the Lord chooses to begin a new era of ministry for these two men. They are "set apart" by the church body for this apostolic ministry. In this case, it is the local elders and congregation that "laid their hands on them and sent them off" (v. 3).

The elements common in both of these events are the following: (1) It is a public ceremony before the whole church; (2) The men are set apart for specific ministry in the church; and (3) The event includes laying on of hands and prayer. These scarce details allow for great flexibility in our own ordination services, but they provide a solid structure to guide us.

EXPRESSIONS OF FELLOWSHIP

(ROM. 16:16; JAMES 2:1-4; 1 PETER 5:14)

A final element of biblical worship is one we can call "expressions of fellowship." This is a kind of catch-all for displays of proper Christian affection and relationship in our meetings. We can include here the "holy kiss" (Rom. 16:16; 1 Peter 5:14). This was a culturally sensitive display of affection that was to be practiced in the church as well. Paul and Peter meant nothing sensual in this phrase, but something like our handshake or maybe the handshake in which a man grabs the right hand of another man while also grabbing the man's right shoulder with his left hand. It is a gesture that conveys our joy in seeing the other person and respect for their place in the body of Christ.

We might also include here the numerous references to "greeting one another" in the New Testament. Paul always includes greetings from those he is with at the time he writes his epistles. In Colossians 4:10 we read that "Aristarchus my fellow prisoner greets you," and in Romans 16:16, "All the churches of Christ greet you." Our affection in the church is not simply to be felt, but it is also to be expressed. The negative example found in James 2:1-4 reminds us that we are to embrace all kinds of people without any "partiality" rooted in class, race, gender, age, dress, occupation, or social standing. This is not to erase differences between people, but we cannot use these as a grounds for judgment. We are to see past these externalities to the character and gifting beneath them.

All of this means that a Sunday service should be a place of a lot of chatter, joy, and warm hospitality. It should have the feel of a family reunion, not the look of a shopping mall—filled with people who care little for anyone other than themselves.

CHURCH DISCIPLINE

(1 TIM. 5:20; MATT. 18:15-20; 1 COR. 5:11)

A final, more sobering, side of our corporate worship is church discipline. Some elders may decide to include this only in members meetings and not the public gathering of the church. Lord willing, this will be relatively uncommon in our church life, but we should not be naïve in thinking that it will never have a place in our local church. The two situations that require this kind of public censure are when a person persists in unrepentant sin (Matt. 18:17), and when an elder refuses to repent of his sin (1 Tim. 5:20). In both situations there is a public rebuke that is to be given before "the church" (Matt. 18:17), "in the presence of all," as it is said in 1 Tim. 5:20.

Such public and dramatic responses are not for any and every sin, or all unrepentant sin. The reality of life in the flesh is that we will continue sinning until the day we die. Indwelling sin remains and plagues us such that we are daily tempted and we daily fall. Certain sins, however, bring such damage to the individual and the church that a more dramatic response is required. Paul mentions some of these in 1 Corinthians 5:11: "anyone who bears the name of brother if he is guilty of sexual immorality or greed, or is an idolater, reviler, drunkard, or swindler—[do] not even...eat with such a one." Titus 3:10 also adds that “a person who stirs up division” should also be removed from the church. For an elder, we can accept charges against him provided these are substantiated ("two or three witnesses," 1 Tim. 5:19) and significant. Likely, such charges relate to the requirements listed in 1 Timothy 3:1-7 and Titus 1:5-9.

For many of us, church discipline and the public rebuke of elders are extremely rare. The critical thing for us is simply to accept that this is indeed a part of New Testament church life. Whether we decide to perform such functions in a typical Sunday service, or we hold a special "members only" meeting is up to the wisdom of the local elders. The fact that these are to be a part of our life together is not; this is a clear command that God has laid down for us in the Word of God.

THE PLACE OF "CHRISTIAN PRUDENCE"

The above list orients us well to what is "prescribed in the Holy Scripture," the foundation and starting point of our corporate worship. As we said, this only starts the process. We must add to this our unique "Christian prudence" to organize our gatherings. What might we say here?

First, Christian prudence helps us establish (and maintain) our priorities. Every worship service presents us with myriad possibilities. We cannot do everything commanded in Scripture at every service. Wisdom helps us to see among the many possibilities those things that are to be our priorities. This is critical because priorities keep us from losing our center and foundation, and they also provide a check for our creativity and imagination. If our artistic ideas result in losing our grip on our priorities, then we know that we need to make a change. The priorities that rise to the surface in the Bible are the six activities of reading and teaching the Scriptures, prayer, corporate singing, offerings, the practice of spiritual gifts, and the Lord's Supper.

Thus, with our Christian prudence, we both incorporate the broader list of worship activities found in the Bible and retain our grip on those that must remain priorities. This affects both the proportions of the different elements in our services, and also helps us over the course of a month or a year to include the whole scope of biblical responses to God's glory.

Second, Christian prudence helps us to navigate through our cultural setting. We live immersed in our culture and affected by it at every turn. To deny this is simply to be naïve. No movement is so counter-cultural that the culture itself does not affect it. The challenge is to discern as much as we can *how* the culture is affecting us. We also need to make decisions in light of our particular setting.

As an example, those of us in the suburban West know that excellence in technology is necessary to retain credibility and to serve our congregations. Technology makes our sermons available on the internet and makes our song lyrics visible as we sing. Technology also keeps our rooms cool in the summer and warm in the winter.

Yet, wisdom is essential here, for just as soon as we take a step toward technology to reach our congregation, we might need to take a step back once we check it against the Bible. We must not be slaves to technological gadgetry but employ technology to reach those who spend their days immersed in a digital world.

To take a modern negative example, the Bible teaches that gifted men are to be raised up to teach God's people in a specific location. This means *actual men*, not *virtual* ones. This is why the trend of "satellite campuses" where a single teacher is broadcast to multiple locations is a disturbing one. Has God failed to provide adequate teachers in the body of Christ? Is the quality of the one teacher so uniquely and incomparably excellent that he must teach at all venues? We are not thinking here of very occasional meetings, but the week-in, week-out practice of some congregations. Prudence must help us answer the question whether this represents an appropriate biblical application of its normative teaching, or a lean toward the culture that will result in a weaker and less-informed church in the future.

Third, Christian prudence helps us to make the numerous small changes required to "build up" the gathered church as much as possible. One of the hallmarks of biblical worship is that it must "build up" the body of Christ (e.g., 1 Cor. 14:26ff.). Without doubt, this is one of the areas that takes some of our hardest and most persistent thinking. We can look at the preaching task to see this worked out.

Paul commands us to "preach the word" (2 Tim. 4:2). A basic grasp on this phrase leads us to say that we are "preaching" and not simply "teaching" or "reading." We also learn here the content of our preaching, which is "the word" and not human, secular wisdom. The task is not to entertain but to "preach the word."

This is only part of the story, however, for now we must consider how our preaching of the Word of God "builds up" our church. Suddenly a whole set of factors comes into play, all of which affect how much a given sermon will "build up" our people: sermon length, the right use of humor, the spiritual maturity and diet of our people, the level of their vocabulary and education (and ours!), the best way to dress, stage lighting, amplification, seating, the heating and cooling of the environment, the time the service starts, how deep we go with exegesis or how light with illustrations and applications, etc. So, while the Word of God gives us the imperative ("preach the word"), our Christian prudence will be employed to shape the application for our particular context.

The need for such wisdom never goes away, for our particular context is always changing as our size increases (or decreases), as changes of leadership occur, as major world events happen (wars, 9-11, presidential elections, natural disasters, etc.), or as the average age of a congregation changes. These and other changes mean that the need to refine and examine our services in light of Scripture is a perennial one. We might not alter our priorities or our list of the key elements of our services, but to accomplish each of these elements takes true leadership and wisdom.

****

This chapter has given us the broad overview of what our corporate worship should include—if not every time, then regularly. A few of these need more specific attention, however. Thus, in the next several chapters we will look further into spiritual gifts, the Lord's Supper, and the issue of how worship is to "build up" our fellow believers.

NOTES

[i] For some excellent examples: D.A. Carson cites the list of Ed Clowney, "Presbyterian Worship," *Worship: Adoration and Action,* ed. D. A. Carson, in *Worship by the Book,* 48; John Frame, *Worship in Spirit and*

Truth (Phillipsburg, New Jersey: Presbyterian and Reformed Publishing Company, 1996), 56-60; Bryan Chapell, *Christ-Centered Worship: Letting the Gospel Shape our Practice* (Grand Rapids, MI: Baker Academic, 2009), 145-146; Allen Ross, Grand Rapids, MI: Kregel Publications, 2006, 415-458.

[ii] While the Lord's Supper will be covered below, baptism is covered elsewhere by the author in *Believe and Be Baptized: Key Truths for Those Considering Baptism* (2011).

CHAPTER FIVE

"Now Concerning Spiritual Gifts..."

INTRODUCTION

It's fair to ask with respect to spiritual gifts, "Why bother with such a controversial and confusing topic?" Yes, it is controversial. The impassioned arguments on all sides of all issues in this arena make that clear. The confusion is equally prominent. Good Christians who regularly read their Bibles often struggle to understand the place of the Holy Spirit in their lives. So again, "Why bother?"

One simple reason is that God has said a great deal about it. He is the God of all creation, the Lord of our lives, and the Savior who died to set us free. If he speaks, we want to listen. And when he speaks *a lot* on a matter, we want especially to listen. Related to that, sometimes with issues of the Christian life it is not the number of texts that are important, but the strength of them. 1 Corinthians 12-14 is so clear, so explicit, and so extensive that we need to let it function in the area that it speaks to: spiritual gifts.

A second reason is the difference the spiritual gifts make in the life of a Christian. They encourage us, strengthen us, and bring us joy when we are suffering. They bring insight when we need direction, even healing when we are sick. Through spiritual gifts we get to make a difference in the lives of others, and others make a difference to us. Through the gifts of the Spirit the very presence of God empowers his people to be a means of grace in the lives of others.

For worship leaders there is a third reason still. 1 Corinthians 12-14 (and we could add chapter 11) provide some of the clearest instruction we have about New Testament church meetings. In fact, in terms of the corporate worship of the early church, there is no rival to this text. That is why it is noteworthy that the point of Paul's discussion in these chapters is the path toward the healthy functioning of the gifts of the Spirit in the gathered church. What did it mean for the apostle Paul when a healthy New Testament church gathered for their corporate worship? It meant that spiritual gifts would be evident, diverse, and orderly. Their absence would not be a sign that a church is functioning in an orderly manner, but that the church is missing out on a crucial element of its worship. Thus, his words there need to find a way into the thinking, planning, and leading of worship leaders.

For these reasons (at least) we need to give attention to 1 Corinthians 12-14 and other passages that speak to the Holy Spirit in the context of our corporate worship. We will first work through the Corinthians text.

SPIRITUAL GIFTS: THE FIRST GIFT (12:1-3)

Paul begins his discussion with a fundamental clarification. Whether someone is "spiritual" or not is not a matter of glossalalia (speaking in tongues) or ecstatic speech or gifts of healing or dynamic prophecies. Someone is "spiritual" if they proclaim, "Jesus is Lord!" and refuse that "Jesus is anathema" (12:3). Thus, an unconverted Jew who would say, "Jesus is anathema," or a pagan who says, "Caesar is Lord," is not "spiritual." Christians, however, are categorically “spiritual.” The clarification is probably addressed more to the charismatics than the non-charismatics (using modern terminology), but Paul digs at both of them in the passage: "Both parties must expand their horizons: the charismatics should not feel they have some exclusive claim on the Spirit, and the non-charismatics should not be writing them off."[i] In other words, if you are a Christian, you are a "charismatic" in the most important sense: You have the Holy

Spirit! Non-charismatics need to hear that charismatics are truly Christians, and that the Spirit is alive in them. Charismatics need to hear that non-charismatics also have the Holy Spirit. The differences are much smaller than what they have in common.

ONE GIVER, MANY GIFTS (12:4-11)

After establishing what being truly charismatic means (being a Christian), Paul then gives us a profound view on the way that God works through a diversity of gifts. As the painter delights in using many colors, the chef a variety of seasonings, so God delights in giving to his people an astonishing variety of gifting. The *source* of these gifts must never be forgotten, however, and neither can their purpose.

12:4-7 begins this section with a refrain of "varieties...the same." The "variety" speaks to the gifts themselves. There are "varieties of gifts...varieties of service...varieties of activities." What God has gifted me to do through the Spirit is unique to me. What God has gifted you to do through his Spirit is unique to you. He is not creating spiritual clones, but wants to display a powerful "variety."

Yet, there is also the drumbeat of "the same": "the same Spirit...the same Lord...the same God who empowers them all in everyone." The "variety" that we observe has a common source and that source is God. It is not the result of mere human leadership or imagination that will give us the variety of gifting that is needed. It is God who brings this variety. The Triune nature of this work is unmistakable in the passage. The Father, the Son, and the Holy Spirit are equally behind all of the gifts, though each plays a slightly different role in their operation. Thus we can see that the *source* of these gifts is the same: God.

12:7 also gives us the common *purpose* for the gifts, though this will be developed much more in chapter 14. He says that "to each is given the manifestation of the Spirit for the common good." "Common good" is better translated as a more vague, "for advantage," and could mean "common good" or "personal gain." In chapter 14, Paul will explore the way the gifts bring “advantage” and “gain” as he shows us that the gifts build us up individually and the whole church as well (14:4). Here he wants us to see that God is giving "to each" a portion of this astounding variety, and he wants us to use our portion.

A sampling of the gifts themselves is given in 12:8-11, a list that has generated enormous debate over the last century. Clearly, Paul wants us to see into some of the "varieties" of gifts and ministries that God gives his people. It is not an exhaustive look at the gifts, however. Most commentators take the list here and the other New Testament lists (Rom. 12:6-8; Eph. 4:11; 1 Peter 4:11; 1 Cor. 12:28) as D.A. Carson does: "No list, including the one immediately before us in 1 Corinthians 12:8-11, is meant to be exhaustive." Yet, while it is not exhaustive, it is significant. The "varieties" of gifts that God gives to his church and even to a specific local church will include *more* than what we find in 12:8-11, but we should expect to find these gifts among them.

A work like this cannot adequately explore the gifts listed in this passage, but we should at least briefly define them. Paul begins by mentioning two speaking gifts, "utterance of wisdom" and "utterance of knowledge." He will mention two additional speaking gifts in verse 10, "prophecy" and "various kinds of tongues." Another speaking role/gift is given in verse 28, "teachers."

One thing obvious by seeing the whole set of speaking gifts is that God inspires his people to speak to one another in a variety of ways. Maybe we can see shades of difference in the "utterance of wisdom" being an insight in applying the Bible in a specific situation, while "utterance of knowledge" could be a person having specific knowledge of a person or situation attributable to the Holy Spirit. "Prophecy" seems to be God speaking to us, while "tongues" is us speaking to God (a difference chapter fourteen explores more fully). A "teacher" could be equivalent to a pastor (cf. Eph. 4:11), but if not, then the role would mean the faithful explanation of the Bible or sound doctrine to the people of God (cf. 1 Tim. 4:6; 2 Tim. 3:16-4:2).

The other gifts are of a different sort: "Faith," "gifts of healing," "the working of miracles," "the ability to distinguish between spirits," and "the interpretation of tongues." "Faith" is not the saving faith possessed by all Christians, but the special faith that hopes in God in dire straits or believes in him for an answer to prayer. Thus, it is akin to the "all faith, so as to remove mountains" in 13:2. "Gifts of healing" is the ability to pray for the sick with unusual success.

Since a miracle is God suspending the normal laws of nature in one way or another, the gift of "miracles" would seem to be our ability to do or pray for such things. In the New Testament the sick are prayed for and healed, but Luke refers to "miracles by the hands of Paul, so that even handkerchiefs or aprons that had touched his skin were carried away to the sick, and their diseases left them and the evil spirits came out to of them" (Acts 19:11-12). It is a nuance to see this as the gift of "miracles" instead of the gift of "healings," but the distinction seems to hold in this instance. Jesus stilling the storm was also a "miracle," as was turning the water into wine (Matt. 8:26; John 2:7-11). So, while the gift of miracles refers to prayers being answered (as with the gifts of faith and healings), the power displayed seems distinctive. Perhaps as well, the interruption of God's normal working in nature is more evident with these situations.

Distinguishing "spirits" means the ability to know when the devil is active behind the scenes in a way different from his general opposition to Christians and to God. "Interpretation of tongues" is the ability to hear another speaking in "tongues" and interpret what is prayed.

The common link in all of these gifts is that God's power becomes active in a specific and unusual manner through the person so gifted. All Christians are to have saving faith and to pray in faith, but the gift of "faith" means this same faith in greater measure. All are to pray for the sick, but those with the "gift of healing" will see an unusual ability to see them delivered from their sickness.

It is clear that while verses 8-11 present many gifts, none of these are explicitly connected to being a musician on a worship team, much less being a worship leader. Two things can be said about that. First, because of the emphasis on "varieties" in this section, we can safely call worship leading a "gift" without risk of going beyond the Bible. Yet, perhaps there is also a challenge to us who serve on worship teams to find a gift within verses 8-11 that we might also exhibit for the sake of blessing our brothers and sisters in the church.

Verse 11 picks up his earlier theme and reminds us that all of the gifts "are empowered by one and the same Spirit, who apportions to each one individually as he wills." The way that God's diversity gets played out in each church and Christian is up to God's sovereign choice. We will later see that some gifts are to be sought by all Christians (14:1), and that love is even more important than the gifts (13:1ff.). What is clear from 12:4-11 is that our Triune God desires to invest his people with a variety of gifts which are meant to be actively used in serving the church. The church will know full maturity and full blessing only as it gives expression to the many gifts that the Lord has given "to each one individually."

ONE BODY, MANY PARTS (12:12-31)

"One Giver, many gifts" in 12:4-11 becomes "One Body, many parts" in 12:12-31. If the single Source of the gifts and the sheer variety of the gifts is the point of 12:4-11, then the inter-relatedness and inter-connection of the gifts is the point of 12:12-31. No part is to function independent of the others. No part is without need of the others. We over-interpret Paul if we try and connect a particular gift to a particular body part—the mouth is the teaching gift, the eye is the prophetic or leadership gift, etc. His metaphor has less ambitious but critical aims. We will highlight two.

The first aim of Paul in these verses is to see that the diversity of the gifts is to have the same cooperation as the parts of our body. This originates in the fact that the body is a single thing. I speak of "my body" and "your body." I am aware that each of our bodies has many parts, but all of these parts constitute a single body.

A body has a great number of parts, and Paul mentions "the foot," "a hand," "the ear," "an eye," and "the sense of smell" (vv. 15-17). He could obviously have added a vast number more, but his point is not a numeric one. His point is that whatever the number of the parts of our body, they all cooperate for the sake of the one "body." A body could not consist of only feet or eyes or hands. It is the variety of parts and their variety of abilities that make it all work.

The second aim of Paul in this section is true humility. This concept of "one body, many parts" has the effect (it should have, anyway) of making me appreciate what God has given to me. I am a *true part* of the body of Christ, a full-fledged member with a special place in his church. Yet, boasting has no place here because I am equally aware that I am only *one part* of the body. Without all of the other parts of the body, I cannot possibly be anything significant. An eye by itself is unimpressive and worthless. A disembodied hand can do nothing. Only as I serve and labor as a part of the whole body of Christ will I see the fruit in my life that God desires.

Paul closes this chapter by bringing the analogy of the body and its parts out of the metaphorical and into the tangible. He says in verse 27 that "you are the body of Christ and individually members of it." In other words, you are a literal "member" of a literal "body," the "body of Christ," which is the church. Through a series of statements and rhetorical questions he gives us a sampling of the "members" of this body. They include the offices of the church: "apostles...prophets...teachers" (v. 28). They also include spiritual gifts: "miracles...gifts of healing, helping, administrating, and various kinds of tongues" (v. 28).

Then he reminds us that individually we do not possess all of these gifts: "Are all apostles? Are all prophets? Are all teachers" (v. 29). The answer to each is, "No." Not all are apostles or teachers or speak in tongues in the corporate meeting. This final paragraph reinforces his "one body, many parts" concept by showing us that it is not merely a metaphor. It is what we are: "You are the body of Christ and individually members of it" (v. 27).

Such a concept of "one body, many parts" has great implications for a worship team and for the corporate worship of the church (some of these will be explored in 14:26ff.). One such implication is that *it does not all depend on me*. I need to play my part as well as I can, but in the end, I am only a part. A time of corporate worship is a whole church moment—a whole body of Christ moment, a time when the whole body is gathering for the purpose of encountering God and encouraging one another. It is prideful and wrong to think that my role is the determining role. It is important, and yet it is not the sole factor that will determine whether God "shows up" or not. I need the whole body to function according to their gifting if we are to accomplish all that God desires for a given setting of worship.

Yet, as important as the spiritual gifts are, there is something more important still. "And I will show you a still more excellent way" (v. 31b). What is this "more excellent way"? It is the way of love.

LOVE IS GREATER THAN THE GIFTS (13:1-13)

Chapter thirteen is one of Paul's most famous chapters in all of his writing. It is read at weddings, stitched into quilts, artistically embedded into greeting cards, and memorized by Christians everywhere. In many ways, the chapter truly stands on its own. Yet, it hits us even more powerfully when we grasp its context. Paul did not send this on a greeting card to the Corinthians. He wrote it in the context of a carefully argued epistle to a struggling church. This becomes clear as we work through his discussion.

The point of chapter thirteen is that love is even greater than the gifts. It is love that is meant to direct, inspire, channel, and ground all of the gifts so that they can accomplish what they are designed for in others and bring the appropriate return to me.

The first paragraph (vv. 1-3) tells us that love is essential. For there to be any gain or life in the spiritual gifts, there must be love. Without love, we become "a noisy gong or a clanging cymbal." Gordon Fee describes such instruments vividly:

> *Although what the former designates is uncertain, at least it is a metaphor for an empty, hollow sound. The latter in fact was an 'instrument' expressly associated with the pagan cults. Perhaps, then, this is an allusion to 12:2 and their former associations with such cults. To speak in tongues as they were doing, thinking that they were 'spiritual' but with no concern for building up the community, is not merely to speak*

> *unintelligible words; it makes one sound like the empty, hollow noises of pagan worship.*[ii]

That is a sobering thought, isn't it, that the absence of love can make our labors on a Sunday morning "sound like the empty, hollow noises of pagan worship." God help us to do what we do *in love.*

Paul's second paragraph (vv. 4-7) shows us what this love will look like. To serve in love is to be "patient" and "not arrogant or rude," "not irritable or resentful." Love is not mere sentimentality, because it "rejoices with the truth." Love stands strong even in the face of obstacles, because "love bears all things, believes all things, hopes all things, endures all things."

Such words remind us that our service as part of a worship team *must be marked by observable Christian love*. My opinions and sense of my own abilities must be carefully checked by love that "does not insist on its own way" (v. 5). When my ideas go unrecognized, I must remember that love "is not irritable or resentful." My relationships with my bandmates should display the love that "bears all things." In the end, I will bring more glory to God by displaying this kind of love than any display of musical excellence.

His third paragraph tells us that love is eternal and therefore preeminent (13:8-13). Love's value has to do with its enduring place in the believer's life. It is permanent and eternal, something that none of the gifts can claim. He speaks of "when the perfect comes," surely the return of Christ who is "the perfect." Fullness, abundance, glorification, and consummation all happen with the return of Christ, not merely the close of the canon as some have unfortunately argued. When Christ the perfect comes and we enter into the new realm of fullness of life with him, spiritual gifts will be unnecessary. Why do we need "gifts of healing" when there is no sickness or death? Why do we need "prophecy" when we shall know all things? (At least, all that glorified, finite creatures *can* know). Why do we need to speak in tongues when we shall talk to God face-to-face? The gifts will disappear in a moment because the need for the gifts will be gone. Even "faith" and "hope" cannot stand up to "love," for they, too, shall cease. Faith will become sight; hope will become possessing what we hoped for.

Paul is by no means telling the Corinthians to soften their practice of spiritual gifts. He merely wants them to do it with a proper emphasis on love. Let there be gifts, but let these gifts be the overflow of a Christian love and practiced within relationships built on Christian love.

MANY GIFTS, ONE PURPOSE: TO BUILD UP THE CHURCH (14:1-40)

To reiterate that Paul wants to modify and not eliminate the practice of the gifts, he opens chapter 14 with an emphatic statement: "Pursue love, and earnestly desire the spiritual gifts, especially that you may prophesy" (v. 1). Chapter fourteen applies the principles of the previous two chapters to the gifts of tongues and prophecy. The key phrase he will use in this chapter is "build up," a translation of the Greek word *oikodomē*. "Build up" is a good translation of this term because it captures what we are to do with the spiritual gifts. Like a house is "built up" by digging its foundation, putting up the framing, and adding a roof, so the spiritual gifts are to bring growth, strength, and structure to other believers. We will encounter this term throughout the chapter.

His discussion centers around the gift of tongues, likely because the Corinthians had an over-emphasis on this gift and apparently an unbridled practice of it. We get the sense that a typical gathering of the Corinthian church would include times where the whole congregation was simultaneously speaking in tongues. Paul's words make the most sense when seen against this kind of backdrop.

His opening verses sound as if he is anti-tongues. He is not. Rather, he is pricking those in the congregation who are obsessed with the gift. They have lost sight of the key point of tongues: "so that the church may be built up" (v. 5). To recapture this side of the gifts they must seek not only *glossalalia*, but also interpretation: "The one who prophesies is greater than the one who speaks in tongues, unless someone interprets, so that the church may be built up" (v. 5).

The first paragraph of the chapter makes several key points. First, while love is "a still more excellent way" (12:31) and we are to "pursue love" (14:1), we are also to "earnestly desire the spiritual gifts" (v. 1). This is a crucial command[iii] to hear. Despite all the potential problems involved with spiritual gifts, Paul in no way wants us to abandon our pursuit of them. We are to "earnestly desire" them.

A second point he makes here is that we are to "especially" desire the gift of prophecy. The reason for this is the impact that prophecy has on us. Where uninterrupted tongues involve a person speaking "to God" (14:2), prophecy "speaks to people for their upbuilding and encouragement and consolation" (v. 3). We are "built up," we are encouraged in difficulty, and we are consoled in our sufferings through the gift of prophecy. Speaking in tongues can have this same impact if the gift is interpreted ("unless someone interprets," v. 5), but without such interpretation we should seek prophecy even more than tongues. Of course, we need to hear such an encouragement in the context of a church that likely has an over-emphasis on the gift of tongues. A church that lacks the gift altogether might hear something quite different.

Our desire to "especially" see the gift of prophecy in a meeting has two key applications for the worship leader. The first is to personally desire and pursue the gift of prophecy for yourself. If we do not function in this gift, we should pray that we do. It is always contagious when the leader on stage functions in such a way.

The second application is to be a means of facilitating this gift in the corporate meeting. Since the gift has such an elevated role in the eyes of Paul, we should think carefully about how to promote the healthy functioning of this gift in our meetings. Maybe occasional reminders are necessary from the worship leader. Maybe more serious teaching is required from the elders. Maybe simple explanations are needed for what a person is to do who thinks they might have a prophecy for the congregation. We will say more about creating an environment for spiritual gifts at the end of the chapter.

The long middle section of the chapter (vv. 6-25) is devoted to a clarification on tongues themselves and to further support the need for interpretation of tongues. They must be interpreted to be understood and achieve their goal (vv. 6-19), and uninterpreted tongues will create the appearance of insanity, not spirituality (vv. 20-25). Paul speaks of his own extensive practice of the gift (v. 18), but says that even "five words" in a known language are better than "ten thousand" where there is no understanding (v. 19). He even adopts the rhetorical device of quoting the Law back to them to show that speaking in unknown languages is historically a sign of God's judgment, not blessing (citing Isa. 28:11 in v. 21). His argument here is to further support the claim that tongues are a wonderful gift for the corporate context *if they are interpreted.*

The third section of the chapter (vv. 26-40) provides several directives for tongues and prophecy in our corporate worship. These chapters are trying to correct excesses within the Corinthian church, but the problem is not the gifts themselves. The problem is the exercise of these gifts. Verses 26-40 direct us in a proper exercise of tongues and prophecy.

Verse 26 is an important verse for our modern context which emphasizes precision, technology, minute-by-minute planning, and professionalism. At times such agendas compete with the perspective we find from Paul: "When you come together, each one has a hymn, a lesson, a revelation, a tongue, or an interpretation." The "each one" of such a verse challenges us to find creative ways to involve members of the congregation in our services. The planned components of our service involve many of them—musicians, ushers, sound and video support, greeters, children's ministry, etc.—but more is being said here. There is also a picture painted of spontaneous contributions from our members. Two concerns are to guide us in this democratic worship: building up and order.

Paul says, "Let all things be done for building up" (v. 26). The test about whether we are achieving a biblical practice of the gifts is whether things are being "done for building up." We should note that this is quite different from Paul saying, "so that no one is personally offended." When the sensibilities of someone are offended this could be a sign of their weakness and immaturity in spiritual gifts, not a sign that our practice is violating the principle of "all things...done for building up." It is critical that we not allow our services to be tyrannized by those with a bias against the gifts. Wise, humble, and most of all, biblical, leadership is required in the area of spiritual gifts. Of course, the caution to those biased toward the gifts is to preserve the commands here to intelligibility, order, and edification.

Verses 27-31 then speak of the order that is to characterize the practice of the gifts. Rather than the entire congregation speaking in tongues simultaneously "two or at most three" are to speak, each with an interpretation. Prophecy is the same: "Let two or three prophets speak." Further, prophecies are to be evaluated. It is possible that Paul envisions a scene in which a prophet speaks to the whole group and then the group weighs what is spoken. Yet, the burden of the text is on the number of speakers ("two or three") and the fact that we "weigh what is said" (v. 29). For tongues, this means that we have an interpretation; for prophecy, this means that we have evaluated the prophecy.

Our own practice involves the speaker saying privately to an elder what they intend for the corporate meeting. The elder is the one to "weigh what is said" in this case. This also allows us to act appropriately if the word is a message in a "tongue." The effect of such order is that "all prophesy one by one" (v. 31), and that "all may learn and all be encouraged." An elder is not required for this role, and a discerning leader could perform this same function. We have simply found it helpful to use elders in this way.

Such concern for building up others and for order means that spontaneous outbursts that disrupt the meeting are out of place. This is the best understanding of Paul saying the "the women should keep silent in the churches" (v. 34). Since he gives instruction in chapter 11 about women praying in churches (11:1-16), it does not seem likely that he means a total "silence." Rather, his concern is "submission, as the Law also says" (14:34).

Paul closes the chapter by bringing several of the themes together: "Earnestly desire to prophesy, and do not forbid speaking in tongues. But all things should be done decently and in order" (vv. 39-40).

Thus, chapter fourteen provides important direction for the practice of spiritual gifts. First, we are to "pursue love, and earnestly desire the spiritual gifts" (v. 1). Second, we are to "let all things be done for building up" (v. 26). Third, our meetings are to be marked by "order" that includes evaluating prophecies and interpreting tongues (vv. 27-32).

HOW SHOULD THIS IMPACT OUR WORSHIP?

Once we have established our convictions from the texts above we still need to think about how this should impact our corporate worship. We will look at only a few issues here, though the implications are myriad.

First, being charismatic is a theological conviction before it is a practical one. What we mean here is that our decision about being charismatic is rooted in what we find in the Bible. Whatever the practical benefits (or difficulties), we begin with the clear teaching of Scripture. This is the foundation on which we are to build, God's blueprint for "God's building" (1 Cor. 3:9). This is a conviction with great practical consequence, but it must begin as a biblical and theological one first.

Second, being charismatic requires as much intentionality as doctrinal faithfulness. We are accustomed to the understanding that doctrinal correctness requires great attention and diligence. Care about expository preaching, efforts to hold classes and seminars, seminaries to train pastors, and a commitment to ongoing study are all part of being doctrinally faithful to the Word of God. Being charismatic requires a similar kind of intentionality. If it is to have a place in our churches, then we will need sermons, classes, leadership, time, and energy committed to this aspect of our corporate life. Just as a marriage requires ongoing work if romance is to be more than a duty, so encountering God in our corporate worship will take a concerted effort on our part.

Third, being charismatic needs to inform how we plan our services and cannot be merely a foundational conviction. Related to our second concern above, being charismatic will need to factor into how we plan our services if it is to be more than a theological conviction. This means that creating "space" is essential. While we will plan our song lists, write out our calls to worship, and plan the flow of the morning, we will still need to allow for space. This includes allowing for time between songs to wait on the Lord. It might seem insignificant, but there can be a great effect by simply waiting before we transition to the next song. The leader might also introduce a time of waiting on the Lord with a few comments: "Let's take a minute to wait on the Lord and silently pray to him." Sometimes with these issues, it is the little difference that makes all the difference.

Fourth, being charismatic should create in us an expectation of God's spontaneous, powerful, and edifying work in our midst. One key element for experiencing the spontaneous work of the Spirit in our midst is having a true expectation that he might actually do this in our meetings. Just as faith-filled prayer can decline into perfunctory prayer, so we can go from true expectation of the Spirit's spontaneous work to assuming he will not work in these ways. At such times, we need to pray for real faith and inform our expectations by the Word of God.

Fifth, being charismatic requires risk that cannot be eliminated. Many of us, including myself, would love a way to be charismatic without all the risk attached. We want to know *for sure* that a word is from God before it is shared publicly. We want to hold off on a spontaneous expression of worship until we have practiced it or informed the band that it is coming. Yet, while it is commendable to rehearse what we can, we must never think that we can eliminate all risk if we want to see God work spontaneously in our meetings. Proverbs 14:4 says, "Where there are no oxen, the manger is clean, but abundant crops come by the strength of the ox." The charismatic can make our mangers pretty messy, but with care and biblical leadership, it can also bring "abundant crops."

CONCLUSION

The people of God are those "who worship by the Spirit of God" (Phil. 3:3). This is a statement of fact, for it defines us as the people of God. Yet, this is also a glorious call to action. God wants us to be continually "filled with the Spirit" personally (Eph. 5:18), and to pursue more of his Spirit to be manifested in our corporate meetings (1 Cor. 14:1). While this is not a call to disorder and emotionalism, there is something here of risk and spontaneity. We are not pursuing mere experience or mere emotion, or equating God's Spirit with either of these. But, there is in these passages a clear expectation that part of being the people born by the Spirit is an experience of that Spirit in a dynamic manner. The radical picture we see in these chapters is that we can encounter God even *today,* and this dimension needs to have a place in our corporate worship. God help us to be biblical, principled, and wise, but also truly charismatic with all of its manifold experiences.

NOTES

[i] D.A. Carson, *Showing the Spirit: A Theological Exposition of 1 Corinthians 12-14* (Grand Rapids, MI: Baker Books, 1987), 26-27.

[ii] *The First Epistle to the Corinthians*, The New International Commentary on the New Testament (Grand Rapids, MI: William B. Eerdmans Publishing Co., 1987), 632.

[iii] In fact, it is a command that is in the imperative mood (mood of command in Greek) and is a present active 2nd person plural verb. In other words, it is a kind of "do this and keep on doing this" command.

CHAPTER SIX

"Do This in Remembrance of Me" The Lord's Supper

INTRODUCTION

All of us want to fully experience God. We want the kind of interaction with God that we enjoy with a friend when we meet them at a coffee shop—seeing his face, hearing his voice, getting immediate reactions to our thoughts, perhaps receiving some tangible assurance about the relationship. The notion of walking by faith and not by sight (2 Cor. 5:7) is not an easy one for us.

In the sacraments, especially in the Lord's Supper, our faith does not become sight, but our faith does get expressed in things that we can see and taste and touch. We, in some sense, see and taste God's assuring love. We get a vivid reminder that our relationship with Christ is not the subject of an archaeological research project, but it is something for this very moment. In the Lord's Supper the event of the cross breaks into our world of sight and sound, and we *experience* the benefits of our redemption. As we will see, it is far more than a mere remembrance.

In our modern setting we can hardly imagine the heated debates surrounding the Lord's Supper that led to great division among the Reformers. Some of this debate had to do with how we do *experience* the risen Christ in the Supper. In what ways is he present or not? Are we eating of his flesh or are we not? Thus, to strengthen our understanding of the Lord's Supper we will take a look at some of the differing views of Luther, Zwingli, Calvin, and the Roman Catholic Church.

The chief part of this chapter, however, will be a look at Matthew and Paul's discussions of the Lord's Supper—Matthew our representative for the synoptic tradition and Paul because his discussion in 1 Corinthians 10-11 provides an extensive look at the Lord's Table. At the end of the chapter we will see how the rest of the New Testament speaks of the Lord's Supper, and then provide some practical reflection to assist in our corporate worship. We begin with a look at Matthew 26:17-30, examining it section by section.

THE PASSOVER

> *Now on the first day of Unleavened Bread the disciples came to Jesus, saying, "Where will you have us prepare for you to eat the Passover?"* [18] *He said, "Go into the city to a certain man and say to him, 'The Teacher says, My time is at hand. I will keep the Passover at your house with my disciples.'"* [19] *And the disciples did as Jesus had directed them, and they prepared the Passover. (Matt. 26:17-19)*

Matthew's record of what has been called The Last Supper opens with two phrases that speak of the same Jewish feast: "the first day of Unleavened Bread" and "the Passover." Throughout the Bible the Passover is the greatest of all the Jewish feasts. We might assume that Yom Kippur, the Day of Atonement (Lev. 16), would surpass it because it brings atonement for the sins of the nation, but it never does. It is the Passover the captures the hearts and minds of the Jewish people more than all other feasts. We can see this in the way that leaders choose to mark times of revival by celebrating the Passover, not the other feasts (e.g., Joshua in Josh. 5:10ff.; Hezekiah in 2 Chron. 30:1ff.).

The roots of the Passover go back to Exodus 12. Following the nine plagues in Egypt God promises a tenth and final plague. This is the death of the firstborn. On a particular night God promises that he will go throughout Egypt "and every firstborn in the land of Egypt shall die, from the firstborn of Pharaoh who sits on the throne, even to the firstborn of the slave girl who is behind the handmill, and all the firstborn of the cattle" (Ex. 11:5).

This judgment of death was an absolute certainty, and yet for the people of God provision was made so that they could escape the judgment. For Israel, the Passover lamb was that provision. They were to put blood from this Passover lamb on "the two doorposts" (Ex. 12:23). It is this blood that brings their redemption: "The blood shall be a sign for you, on the houses where you are. And when I see the blood, I will pass over you, and no plague will befall you to destroy you, when I strike the land of Egypt" (Ex. 12:13).

This first Passover was to be remembered through an annual celebration throughout the history of Israel. They were never to forget this moment of deliverance when the Lord both judged their enemies and accomplished their redemption.

The annual celebration would include specific foods and a message of redemption. The foods were most importantly the "lamb...without blemish, a male a year old" (Ex. 12:5), but also "unleavened bread and bitter herbs" (v. 8). These they were to "eat it in haste" in remembrance of the urgency of that first night (v. 11).

The message of redemption was short but powerful. It was crafted for a day when the Israelites were in the promised land with children who had no remembrance of that first Passover. God commanded them to make known to their children the meaning of this annual feast:

> *And when you come to the land that the LORD will give you, as he has promised, you shall keep this service.* 26 *And when your children say to you, 'What do you mean by this service?'* 27 *you shall say, 'It is the sacrifice of the LORD's Passover, for he passed over the houses of the people of Israel in Egypt, when he struck the Egyptians but*

> *spared our houses.'" And the people bowed their heads and worshiped. (Ex. 12:25-27)*

Israel was never to forget the connection between their annual feast and when the Lord "passed over the houses of the people of Israel in Egypt, when he struck the Egyptians but spared our houses." Parents were to keep this gospel message alive in their families. Even from this brief description it is easy to see why Jesus would pick this feast of all feasts to introduce a sacrament for the people of God that would call them back to their moment of deliverance.

The Passover language from Moses highlights also that the Lord's Supper is a *sign and seal.* Such language comes from Romans 4:11 where Paul is speaking of Abraham's circumcision: "He received the sign of circumcision as a seal of the righteousness that he had by faith while he was still uncircumcised."

The "sign" is the physical act, the tangible part of the action or thing. Circumcision is thus a sign. This "sign" becomes a "seal" when we do it by faith. "Seal" in this case means something like a seal of approval that says the item is the genuine article, that it has been examined and is authentic. Thus, the "seal" means a physical or visible thing that implies something invisible.

My wedding ring is a similar kind of "seal." My ring is a physical sign that I have married someone, Anne Sasser (now Baker) to be specific. The ring itself accomplishes nothing. It is only because that ring is matched to my wedding vows given in December of 1995 that the ring has real significance. Because this "sign" is indeed combined with vows I made it is also a "seal" that says, "This man is indeed truly married." The ring does not make me married, it only communicates to others that I am married. In fact, it is really a double statement because it also says that Anne Sasser made vows to me in return.

Like the annual Passovers in Israel, the Lord's Supper is a "sign," a physical and visible act. When it is combined with my faith and God's work of the Spirit in my conversion, then it is also a "seal," an indicator that I am Christ's and he is mine. More specifically it communicates that I have a share in the cross of

Christ and the benefits of his work of redemption are mine. It is a seal *toward* God that says, "Christ is my Savior," and it is a seal *from* God that says, "You are my child." John Calvin speaks of this seal from God in this way:

> *God has received us, once for all, into his family, to hold us not only as servants but as sons. Thereafter, to fulfill the duties of a most excellent Father concerned for his offspring, he undertakes also to nourish us throughout the course of our life. And not content with this alone, he has willed, by giving his pledge, to assure us of this continuing liberality.*[i]

We are "not only…servants," but we are "sons" of God. Our heavenly Father desires to "nourish us throughout…our life," and thus to "assure us." He does this partially through the Lord's Supper, which he calls the Father's "pledge" to us. Thus, for those already converted by faith, The Lord's Supper becomes another way that God speaks his promises to our soul. We close this section by citing the Heidelberg Catechism:

> ***Question 79.*** *Why then doth Christ call the bread "his body", and the cup "his blood," or "the new covenant in his blood"; and Paul the "communion of body and blood of Christ"?*
> ***Answer:*** *Christ speaks thus, not without great reason, namely, not only thereby to teach us, that as bread and wine support this temporal life, so his crucified body and shed blood are the true meat and drink, whereby our souls are fed to eternal life; (a) but more especially by these visible signs and pledges to assure us, that we are as really partakers of his true body and blood by the operation of the Holy Ghost as we receive by the mouths of our bodies these holy signs in remembrance of him; (b) and that all his sufferings and obedience are as certainly ours, as*

if we had in our own persons suffered and made satisfaction for our sins to God.[ii]

The Passover celebration during the time of Christ evolved from this original meal. The meal would have been celebrated on the 15th day of the month called Nisan, comparable to March/April in our calendar.[iii]

The meal would begin with the head of the household offering thanks and praying over the first of four cups of wine: "Blessed art thou, O Lord God, King of the Universe, who hast brought bread from the earth."[iv] The leader would then explain the unleavened bread, and a course of greens and herbs would follow. It would have been here that Jesus said, "This is my body," over the bread.

Then a boy would ask the meaning of the meal in accordance with Exodus 12:26, and the leader would explain its significance. After this one or two of the Hallel would be sung.

The Hallel is a special set of Psalms used for this night in particular. These included Psalms 113-118. The flow of these Psalms seems particularly appropriate for such an occasion. Psalms 113-114 call us to celebrate the name of the Lord. Psalms 115-116 remind us of different aspects of the Exodus. 116:12-13 even says, "What shall I render to the LORD for all his benefits to me? I will lift up the cup of salvation and call on the name of the LORD." Psalms 117-118 speak of the love and redemption of the Lord, even including the prophetic word on "the stone that the builders rejected" that became "the cornerstone" (v. 22); and, "Blessed is he who comes in the name of the LORD!" (v. 26).

After the psalm (or two) is sung the second cup of wine would have been drunk and then the main course eaten (the Passover lamb). A third cup of wine would then follow, the so-called "cup of blessing." This blessing would be, "Blessed art thou, O Lord God, King of the Universe, who bringeth forth fruit from the vine." Hughes Old tells us that the "blessing goes on to mention the covenant with Abraham and the gift of the promised land. It gives thanks for the kingdom of David and God's covenant with David."[v] Likely here would have been when Jesus said, "This is my blood," over the wine. At this point the rest of the Hallel would have been sung and a fourth cup of wine drunk.

It is clear that this meal was lengthy and involved significant preparation, though not elements difficult to obtain or afford. This is what would have been in view when the disciples "prepared the Passover" (Matt. 26:19).

THE BREAD AND ITS CONTROVERSY

> *Now as they were eating, Jesus took bread, and after blessing it broke it and gave it to the disciples, and said, "Take, eat; this is my body." (26:26)*

We come now to the central part of the Lord's Supper, the bread and the wine, where Jesus calls us to turn from the Passover to his coming crucifixion—our redemption. The "bread" that Jesus takes is likely the ceremonial unleavened bread used at every Passover meal. As we said above, it seems likely this statement by Jesus would have occurred after the first cup of wine and its accompanying blessing (note that "after blessing it" Jesus "broke" the bread). Now instead of the leader of the supper using the bread to look back at the Egyptian Exodus, Jesus is looking ahead to his death, something made more specific in the longer version of Luke: "This is my body, which is given for you" (22:19).

It is at this point that we need to touch on the controversies that have surrounded these texts. The sentences that have produced the debate are, "This is my body," and, "This is my blood of the covenant" (v. 28). We can even say more precisely that the history of the church has been profoundly affected by the word "is" in these two sentences.

The three main views on these sentences are the Roman Catholic, the Lutheran, and the Zwinglian. Most denominations today align themselves with the Zwinglian view, but of course, the number of Roman Catholics and Lutherans in the world is significant.

The Roman Catholic view holds that when Jesus says, "This is my body," when speaking of the bread that he meant the bread was literally his "body." It is as concrete as if I lift up my laptop to you and say, "This is my laptop." In all subsequent celebrations of the Lord's Supper they would argue that this holds true as well. Thus, the bread itself actually changes in substance with the celebration of the Lord's Supper—hence the term *transubstantiation*—so that the priest in our contemporary setting can also say, "This is the body of Christ," and it is literally the case. The Council of Trent in 1551 articulated transubstantiation as the "conversion" of the bread and wine into the body and blood of Christ: "our Lord Jesus Christ, true God and man, is truly, really, and substantially contained under the species of those sensible things."[vi] Even more problematic is their defense in 1562 of the Lord's Supper as a re-sacrifice of the body and blood of Christ that is actually a "propitiatory sacrifice."[vii]

Their views did not originate overnight in the 4th century, but was a step-by-step loss of the original sense of the Lord's Supper and more importantly, the finished work of the cross. The Dutch theologian Herman Bavinck says, "Gradually the difference between the Old and the New Testament dispensation was lost. The gathering place was changed into a temple, the minister became a priest, the Lord's Supper a sacrifice, and the table an altar."[viii]

Martin Luther originally held the view that the bread and wine were "signs and pledges of the forgiveness of sins secured by Christ's death and received by faith,"[ix] but as the Reformation scuffles continued about the Lord's Supper he changed. Eventually he would hold that "the body of Christ…is realistically and substantially present in, with, and under [the elements of the] Lord's Super. He saw this as being analogous to the presence of Christ's divine nature in his human nature and as heat is or can be present in iron."[x] His view, termed *consubstantiation,* was captured in the 1530 Augsburg Confession:

> *The Tenth Article has been approved, in which we confess that we believe, that in the Lord's Supper the body and blood of Christ are truly and substantially present, and are truly tendered, with those things which are seen, bread and wine, to those who receive the Sacrament.*[xi]

Despite the number of adherents to these two positions, the Roman Catholic and the Lutheran views must be rejected because *they violate the doctrine of Christ.* The apostle Peter tells us clearly *where* Christ is: "Jesus Christ...has gone into heaven and is at the right hand of God, with angels, authorities, and powers having been subjected to him" (1 Peter 3:21, 22). He is somewhere right now, but that somewhere is not in the celebrations of the Lord's Supper around the globe. He is, in fact, "at the right hand of God." Further, the Bible is clear that from this location he will come again. He will descend in all of his radiant glory to establish God's kingdom on earth at the consummation (Rev. 19:11ff.; etc.).

Second we consider how Christ is indeed present with us. Passages like Matthew 28:20 remind us of Christ's *omnipresence*: "I am with you always, to the end of the age." Thus, we must affirm Christ's omnipresence through the Holy Spirit even as we affirm his bodily presence "at the right hand of God." He is with us and even in us as the people of God, but this is not how Roman Catholics and Lutherans affirm his presence in the Supper. Instead they are arguing for his *physical* presence. That is why their views must be rejected as unsupportable by the New Testament.

The third dominant view of the Lord's Supper had an early defender in Ulrich Zwingli. He held that Christ was speaking figuratively when he said, "This is my body," and, "This is my blood." The bread and wine remain bread and wine in every way before, during, and after the Lord's Supper. Christ is present by his Spirit, but remains "at the right hand of God" physically. Zwingli said that "To eat the body of Christ spiritually is nothing other than to rest, in one's spirit and mind, in the compassion and goodness of God through Christ." [xii] Therefore, as Bavinck says,

> *In the Lord's Supper, accordingly, we confess our faith and express what Christ continually means to us by faith and what we enjoy of him. And we do this in remembrance of Christ, to proclaim and give thanks for his benefits.*[xiii]

Most Presbyterian and Baptist confessions and theology are represented by this view, often called the *memorial* view of the Lord's Supper.

The essence of this view is that when we eat physically of the bread and drink the cup we are feasting on Christ by faith. While he remains bodily in heaven we are eating and drinking by faith and receiving him internally by means of the Holy Spirit. There is therefore a real effect on us when we "partake of Christ through faith" by eating the Lord's Supper, but it is not because of any physical presence of Christ. It is instead a confession of "our faith" and something we do "in remembrance of Christ, to proclaim and give thanks for his benefits."

Thus, as with singing worship songs, hearing the Word of God preached, or praying, when we consider in true faith the crucifixion and redemption of our Savior, our souls and minds can "rest...in the compassion and goodness of Christ." That is the great and special benefit of the Lord's Supper. As Wayne Grudem says, "Today most Protestants would say, in addition to the fact that the bread and wine symbolize the body and blood of Christ, that Christ is also *spiritually present* in a special way as we partake of the bread and wine."[xiv] Because he is "spiritually present in a special way," we celebrate the Lord's Supper in faith, joy, gratitude, and worship. The Westminster Confession calls it a "commemoration of that one offering of Himself" (29.2) and says that

> *worthy receivers, outwardly partaking of the visible elements, in this sacrament, do then also, inwardly by faith, really and indeed, yet not carnally and corporally but spiritually, receive, and feed upon, Christ crucified, and all benefits of His death: the body and blood of Christ being then, not corporally or carnally, in, with, or under the bread and wine; yet, as really, but spiritually, present to the faith of believers in that ordinance, as the elements themselves are to their outward sense (29:7).*

The language is difficult, but the point is that just as the elements are physical before our "outward" senses, so is the body and blood of Christ "really, but spiritually, present to the faith of believers" in the Supper.

THE WINE

> *And he took a cup, and when he had given thanks he gave it to them, saying, "Drink of it, all of you, [28] for this is my blood of the covenant, which is poured out for many for the forgiveness of sins.(Matt. 26:27-29)*

After Jesus and the disciples had drunk the second cup of wine and eaten the main course (lamb, herbs), they would have drunk the cup of blessing. It seems most likely that here is where Jesus would have said, "This is my blood."

Our familiarity with Jesus' statement might rob us of some of the dramatic impact it would have had on these pious Jews. The notion of drinking blood, as Jesus is commanding here even if symbolically, would have been deeply offensive to a Jewish audience. Pagans and cannibals had their own tradition with this practice, but certainly not Jews.

> *The idea would have been unthinkable to a Jew, for whom the consumption of any blood was strictly forbidden. Yet now the disciples, who have just been invited to "eat Jesus' body," are also invited to "drink Jesus' blood." Long familiarity with Eucharistic language has blunted the profoundly shocking nature of this imagery, which conjures up ideas of both human sacrifice and cannibalism, as well as overriding the Mosaic taboo on consuming blood.*[xv]

Matthew records that they drank this cup only after Jesus "had given thanks." The word for "giving thanks" is from *eucharisteō*, and this is the reason the Lord's Supper is called the *Eucharist* in many traditions (Anglican, etc.). Of course, calling it a *Eucharist* does not mean that the important element is Jesus' giving thanks, but that central to the Lord's Supper is *our giving thanks* for this greatest of all gifts given to us. If we are to give thanks "in all things" (1 Thess. 5:18) and "for all things" (Eph. 5:20), then surely we are to give thanks "to God for his inexpressible gift" (2 Cor. 9:15).

Two things are said here that highlight the significance of Jesus' blood. Jesus first calls it, "my blood of the covenant." As we saw in chapter three it is "the new covenant" of Jeremiah 31:31-34 that is in view here. Just as the covenant at Mt. Sinai (the old covenant under Moses) was inaugurated by Moses sprinkling blood "on the people" (Ex. 24:8), so the new covenant would begin only with the offering of Jesus' blood. For Jesus to speak of this covenant means that all the great promises contained in the new covenant would begin once his redemption was offered (his death, burial, resurrection, ascension, sending of the Spirit). God's law is on our hearts, we possess a true knowledge of him, and our sins are completely, eternally forgiven. All of this is communicated in Jesus saying, "This is my blood of the covenant."

The second statement regarding his blood that Jesus makes tells us that it is "poured out for many for the forgiveness of sins" (v. 28). R. T. France explains why it is significant that Jesus says "for many" in this description:

> *"Poured out for many" recalls the 'many' who are repeatedly referred to in Isa. 53:11-12 as the beneficiaries of the suffering and death of the servant of God, an allusion already familiar to us from 20:28, where again it was specifically linked to the purpose of Jesus' death; here the Isa. 53 allusion is further suggested by the verb 'poured out,' which is used in Isa. 53:12 of the servant 'pouring out his life to death.'"*[xvi]

In other words, to say, "poured out for many," is a shorthand way of saying, "I am the Suffering Servant of Isaiah 53 who is offering myself to achieve all that is promised there." Isaiah 53 vividly presents the Substitute bearing our sins as a guilt offering, a sacrifice that would "make many to be accounted righteous" (v. 11) as he bears their sins and intercedes "for the transgressors" (v. 12).

Jesus finishes his sentence by making his accomplishment clear: "the forgiveness of sins." What does Jesus accomplish by his sacrifice of atonement? "The forgiveness of sins." The sins that separate us from the Lord, wreck all of our relationships, darken our minds and hearts, and could potentially build up for us an eternity of judgment are "forgiven" because of the shed blood of Jesus Christ. Without his blood there is no forgiveness of sins. Without the sacrifice of Christ we would all die in our sins without any hope for redemption. All forgiveness in the Old Testament anticipates the work of Christ, and all forgiveness in the New Testament is grounded in the work of Christ: "In him we have redemption through his blood, the forgiveness of our trespasses, according to the riches of his grace" (Eph. 1:7).

Thus, in this single statement are brought together three strands of OT teaching: the covenant at Sinai (Ex. 24:8), the promise of a new covenant (Jer. 31:31-34), and the substitutionary atonement of the Suffering Servant (Isa. 53). All of these gloriously unite at the cross of Christ where Jesus sheds his own blood to inaugurate the new covenant and bring the definitive forgiveness of sins. All of these unite in this simple act of drinking the cup of the Lord.

THE KINGDOM AND THE DEPARTURE

> *"I tell you I will not drink again of this fruit of the vine until that day when I drink it new with you in my Father's kingdom." And when they had sung a hymn, they went out to the Mount of Olives. (26:29-30)*

The final statement by Jesus looks beyond the near-term of the cross and extends our gaze far ahead. He looks to that day when all is fulfilled and Jesus and his people enjoy "the marriage supper of the Lamb" (Rev. 19:9). Before that time Jesus will not drink with his disciples. Surely they could not have discerned how true was his meaning. Jesus was confirming that he had reached the end of his incarnate ministry as the un-glorified Christ. At his death and resurrection he would be transformed into the incarnate Christ who is also glorified. Yet, that was no consummation. The consummation was far ahead—humanly speaking, of course. Thus, while we have our eyes on the cross at the Lord's Supper, there is in it an anticipation of that day when all of us shall celebrate with Jesus "in my Father's kingdom."

As the meal is now complete and the instruction has been given, "they…sung a hymn." Likely they completed the remainder of the Hallel. One can even imagine Jesus singing Psalm 118:

The stone that the builders rejected
Has become the cornerstone.
This is the LORD's doing;
It is marvelous in our eyes. (vv. 22-23)

Leaving the room where the Passover was held they journey to the Mount of Olives where Jesus would agonize in prayer to his Father and then be arrested. The night would not end, however, until he had already been tried by the Jewish leaders and found guilty of the capital crime of blasphemy. What Jesus anticipated and explained in the Lord's Supper would thus come to pass within twenty-four hours.

This concludes Matthew's presentation of the Lord's Supper. To give us a clear picture of the Lord's Supper it seemed best to work through a single account and offer reflections upon it. Now, however, we need to see what the rest of the New Testament reveals about the Lord's Supper. We will begin with Paul's words to the Corinthians because outside of the synoptics this is the most significant statement about the Lord's Supper made in the New Testament.

1 CORINTHIANS 10:1-22; 11:17-34

1 Corinthians 10 and 11 add to our view of the Lord's Supper. Paul's speaks in 1 Corinthians 10 of various aspects of meat sacrificed to false gods. Paul sees temptations all around the issue and wants to help the Corinthians navigate these treacherous

waters. There are both freedoms and restrictions, with freedoms dominating the end of the chapter (10:23-31) and restrictions the beginning. It is the first part of the chapter (10:1-22) that speaks of the Lord's Supper.

In these verses Paul is arguing against a specific practice in the Corinthian church. Apparently, many were eating in pagan temples, perhaps not for religious reasons but for social ones. Either way, Paul sees this as dangerous and sinful, but why? The key is his notion of *participation.* That is, when they eat and drink at pagan temples there is a sense in which they are "participants with demons" (v. 20). The Greek word for "participation" throughout the passage is *koinōnia,* a word that is often "fellowship" (Acts 2:42) or "partnership" (Phil. 1:5). Thus, to eat or drink at a pagan temple brings us into a kind of *fellowship* or *partnership* with those demons. In this way we are "participants with demons" (v. 20).

We are instead to reserve such ceremonial/religious eating and drinking for the Lord's Supper. In the Lord's Supper we drink as "a participation in the blood of Christ," and we eat as "a participation in the body of Christ" (v. 16). This is like "the people of Israel" where "those who eat the sacrifices" are "participants in the altar" (v. 18). Paul then makes the statement to which the whole chapter is leading: "You cannot drink the cup of the Lord and the cup of demons. You cannot partake of the table of the Lord and the table of demons" (v. 21).

The vividness of the participation language adds a critical dimension to our understanding of the Lord's Supper. It means that while it is right to highlight the "remembrance" component of the Supper (Luke 22:19; 1 Cor. 11:24-25), we must not reduce this remembering to a mere act of our minds. I can "remember" a high school math class I once took, but to "participate" in a math class today would be a whole other matter! By faith exercised in the Supper we are once again "participating" in the glorious covenant of grace that Christ accomplished through his suffering. The forgiveness of sins and knowledge of God that the covenant established I experience afresh as I participate in the body and blood of Christ.

SACRAMENT, SIGN, AND SEAL

Such "participation" is hard to fully understand. In theological studies it touches on the concept of a "sacrament," and especially the "objectivity of the sacraments." That is, in what way do the bread and wine actually (objectively) communicate grace? Is it entirely objective and so indifferent to whether I exercise my faith or not? (the Roman Catholic view). Or is it no different from any other moment when I exercise my faith in the person and work of Christ and so receive his benefits? (purely memorial view).

The "participation" language of 1 Corinthians 10 pushes us beyond a purely memorial view and says that grace is imparted in the elements (bread and wine, bread and juice). Yet, just as eating the manna in the wilderness and walking through the Red Sea were to be done with a deep awareness of God's provision through it all (1 Cor. 10:1-5), so our eating is to be a physical act done *in faith*. The faith takes the physical act and turns it into a means of grace.

Herman Bavinck uses the analogy of the Word of God.[xvii] When the Word of God is preached, that physical act of communicating the truth of Scripture accomplishes nothing in a heart unless the Holy Spirit is active in that heart and faith is being exercised by that person. Apart from God's activity and the presence of faith, the preaching of the Word is an ineffective and purely physical (i.e., not spiritual) action.

Thus, it is the activity of God upon the individual and the faith exercised by that individual that make the Lord's Supper accomplish anything at all. When these are present the Lord's Supper becomes a powerful way that we experience the blessings of the cross of Christ—in a way akin to our fresh experience of the same benefits when we respond to the Word preached:

> *In the Word, Christ is truly and essentially offered and granted to everyone who believes. And he is just as really communicated to believers in the sacrament. The sacrament grants the same full Christ as the Word and in the same manner, that is, a spiritual manner by faith, even though the*

means differ, one being audible and the other visible.[xviii]

All of this means that real grace is imparted through the Lord's Supper, but *only* when it is matched to faith in the recipient. Apart from such faith the Supper does not work in the heart of the individual worshiper.

1 CORINTHIANS 11:17-34

As Paul's discussion in 1 Corinthians continues in 11:17-34 he returns to the topic of the Lord's Supper in a much more direct manner. While there is much overlap here with what we have already seen, he also adds several new elements.

First, the Lord's Supper is to be a picture of the unity of an entire local church. He speaks of their divisions "when you come together" (vv. 17-18). This verb, "come together," is used extensively throughout this part of 1 Corinthians and nowhere else in the New Testament outside of the gospels and Acts (23 occurrences in the gospels and Acts). Yet, here we find it seven times (11:17, 18, 20, 33, 34; 14:23, 26).

This demonstrates first *when* the Lord's Supper occurs: it occurs when the church *came together*. We see, then, that the ceremony is one practiced by the whole church together, not being done in small group settings or in ad-hoc situations.

The use of this verb teaches us second what the Lord's Supper *means*: it is a picture of the church *coming together,* its unity as the body of Christ. Paul said in 10:17, "Because there is one bread, we who are many are one body, for we all partake of the one bread." Thus, the unity of the church is to be communicated in the practice of the Lord' Supper. That is why their divisions virtually eliminated the significance of the Lord's Supper: "When you come together, it is not the Lord's Supper that you eat" (11:20). Unity in the church and the Lord's Supper are to be intimately connected.

Second, Paul speaks of the Supper as a "meal" (v. 21). In addressing the class distinctions appearing in the Supper, he gives us a hint about how it was originally practiced. At the end of the chapter he will tell everyone to "eat at home" if you are hungry so that you will be able to wait for all to arrive at the Supper (11:33-34). This last comment helps us see that the early practice of the Lord's Supper involved much more than a token amount of bread. In fact, so much food is apparently eaten at these gatherings that to miss it is to go "hungry."

Third, Paul continues the tradition established by Jesus at the Last Supper (11:23-26). In this paragraph Paul reminds the Corinthians of what he "delivered" to them, a tradition he "received from the Lord" (v. 23). His verses read closest to Luke 22:19-20. Perhaps it was through Luke himself that Paul received this tradition, for Luke traveled with Paul extensively (e.g., Acts 27:1).

Fourth, the Lord's Supper is proclaiming "the Lord's death until he comes" (11:26). As in the synoptics that mention the coming kingdom of the Lord, so Paul sees in the Lord's Supper an eschatological hope. We "do this in remembrance" of the Lord's death, but only "until he comes." After Christ returns we will remember his death, but not through the Lord's Supper. It is a rite that we practice in this epoch, one where we both cling to the cross in the past and anticipate his return in the future. The Lord's Supper does both.

Fifth, the Lord's Supper must not be eaten "in an unworthy manner" or we risk experiencing the discipline of the Lord (11:27-32). The elevation of the cross of Christ that happens in the Lord's Supper has implications, and one of these is that we must eat it in a worthy manner. Anyone who does not "will be guilty concerning the body and blood of the Lord" (v. 27). It would appear that the apostle sees the divisiveness of the Corinthians as utterly inconsistent with the Lord's Supper. One cannot speak of the crucified body of Christ with such a poor view of the church as "the body of Christ" (1 Cor. 12:27). The Supper is meant to communicate both our union with Christ and our unity as his people. When all we bring is disunity to the Supper, we are not "discerning the body" (11:29) and we therefore drink "judgment" on ourselves. Paul says this is why some are experiencing the physical discipline of the Lord: "Many…are weak and ill, and some have died" (v. 30).

SUMMARY ON THE LORD'S SUPPER

Because this discussion has been so extensive it will help to now offer a summary of what we covered. Any one of these points could provide an excellent focus for a given celebration of the Lord's Supper.

The Lord's Supper connects us to the Passover lamb of the Old Testament (1 Cor. 5:7; Mark 14:12ff.; Luke 22:7ff.; Ex. 12). Jesus redefines the Passover as he leads the disciples through this meal, but it is significant that he chooses this particular rite to be continued in this new manner. In the lamb slaughtered to save the Israelites from death (Ex. 12:7-13) we find a vivid picture of "the Lamb of God, who takes away the sin of the world" (John 1:29).

The Lord's Supper highlights Jesus inaugurating the new covenant for us through his death (Luke 22:20; 1 Cor. 11:25; Jer. 31:31-34). As blood was sprinkled to inaugurate the old covenant (Ex. 24:8), so blood is shed to inaugurate the new covenant, only this time it was the blood of God's own Son. The new covenant means a true knowledge of God and true forgiveness of sin.

The Lord's Supper reminds us that Jesus is the Suffering Servant of Isaiah 53 (Matt. 26:28; Isa. 53:11-12). Jesus saying that his blood is offered "for many" connects us to the "many...accounted righteous" in Isaiah 53:11 through laying on him "the iniquity of us all" (Isa. 53:6).

The Lord's Supper confirms that the people of God are to remain gospel-centered (1 Cor. 2:2; 2 Tim. 3:8; 1 Cor. 11:26). The Lord's Supper is to be practiced until Christ returns, and thus the people of God are never to lose sight of the cross in their lives and corporate worship.

The Lord's Supper is an emphatic statement that our sins have been forgiven (Matt. 26:28; Eph. 1:7; Heb. 9:22). Implied in our discussion above is the sense that when we celebrate the Lord's Supper we have a profound and powerful demonstration that our sins have been forgiven. This would make songs of joy entirely appropriate after we partake of the elements.

We are to bring both sobriety and celebration to the Lord's Supper (1 Cor. 11:26). There is a dual emphasis in this ceremony, for it highlights both the reality of our sin which required the death of Christ, and the certainty of our forgiveness and sonship which was purchased eternally by that same death.

The Lord's Supper is to be a corporate event (1 Cor. 11:17, 18, 20, 33, 34). It would appear from 1 Corinthians 11:17-34 that we are to practice this rite when the church "comes together," and presumably this means the entire church. This is partly because the Lord's Supper symbolizes not just our salvation in Christ, but also the unity that we possess as "the body of Christ."

We are to eat the Lord's Supper in a worthy manner (1 Cor. 11:27ff.). The key element to bring to the Table is faith. We are never to eat and drink without an active faith that once again rests in the sacrifice of Christ and once again recalls his merciful grace poured out for us. Whether this faith feels conviction over sin or deeper joy in Christ's forgiveness or more determination to be unified with our Christian brothers and sisters will depend on our situation. Faith can express itself in any number of ways that mark our eating and drinking as "worthy."

We are actually "participating" in Christ's death when we eat and drink, not simply "remembering" (1 Cor. 10:16-22). When we "remember" Christ's death through eating and drinking there is a sense in which we are participating once again in that death. This does not mean that Christ is being re-sacrificed or that I am being re-converted, both of which are once-for-all-time events. It means that I am receiving fresh grace from God as I commune with him, assure my soul of his forgiveness, and declare to him that he is my God and Father.

The Lord's Supper is a sacramental sign that is a "seal" of the forgiveness I have received in Christ and the sacrifice that he made on my behalf (Rom. 4:11; Matt. 26:26-28). The Table of the Lord is a proclamation that God has adopted me as his own and poured out his forgiveness and mercy over me, and that I have a share in the benefits of the redemptive work of Christ.

PRACTICAL CONCERNS

Finally, we need to consider a few practical concerns. There are many that we could add, but we will leave those for the worship leaders and the elders of a local church to work out.

Should an elder lead the Meal? While many traditions hold to this, we do not get from the Bible a mandate that the Lord's Supper must be led by an officer in the church. There is a logic and practical benefit to this, but no biblical requirement. Certainly a church's practice of the Meal will reflect the leadership and teaching of its elders, however.

How often should it be practiced? All that we know from the Bible is that when it is practiced, it should be done rightly. The frequency of references to the Supper in comparison with other aspects of new covenant worship should provoke us in the direction of 'more often' rather than 'less often,' but whether this means quarterly (as in Calvin's Geneva), monthly (as in many evangelical churches), weekly (as in many 'high church' traditions), or some other rotation is for us to decide in our own setting.

Should we use real bread and real wine? The Bible does not reveal a special significance about the wine being served at the table. The bread was intentionally "unleavened." Many traditions use grape juice, a kind of modern "fruit of the vine." The Bible provides no mandate here, though wisdom would seem to point us toward using bread and drink that do not conjure up shallow or unhelpful images (i.e., we would not use Twinkies and Coke, for instance). There are many practical concerns that impact a church celebrating the Lord's Supper. Perhaps a test for us could be, "Does it help people engage again in the cross of Christ?" or, "Does it allow the best compromise between logistical concerns and spiritual ones?"

****

The Lord's Supper is a simple act with astounding implications. The Bible helps us to see the bread and the cup in kaleidoscopic fashion—a dizzying array of truths all springing from the most pedestrian of elements. God help us to bring some of this richness to all of our celebrations of the Lord's Supper.

NOTES

[i] *Institutes of the Christian Religion,* trans. by Ford Lewis Battles, Vol. 4, 17:1.

[ii] Obtained from http://www.reformed.org/documents/index.html?mainframe=http://www.reformed.org/documents/heidelberg.html on July 27, 2011.
[iii] This overview for the 1st century practice of the Lord's Supper comes from D.A. Carson, *Matthew*, The Expositor's Bible Commentary, Vol. 8, ed. Frank E. Gaebelein (Grand Rapids, MI: The Zondervan Corporation), 533. Hughes Oliphant Old also provides assistance throughout (*Worship: Reformed According to Scripture*).
[iv] Hughes Oliphant Old, *Worship: Reformed According to Scripture* (Louisville, KY: Westminster John Knox Press, 2002), 112.
[v] *Reformed According to Scripture*, 113.
[vi] Obtained from http://www.thecounciloftrent.com/ch13.htm on April 5, 2014.
[vii] The Council of Trent, Session 22 (Obtained from http://www.thecounciloftrent.com/ch22.htm on April 5, 2014).
[viii] *Reformed Dogmatics: Holy Spirit, Church, and New Creation*, Vol. 4, trans. by John Vriend (Grand Rapids, MI: Baker Academic, 2008), 566.
[ix] Ibid., 556.
[x] Ibid.
[xi] Obtained from http://bookofconcord.org/defense_8_holysupper.php on June 24, 2011.
[xii] *Reformed Dogmatics*, Vol. 4, 557.
[xiii] *Reformed Dogmatics*, Vol. 4, 557.
[xiv] *Systematic Theology: An Introduction to Biblical Doctrine* (Grand Rapids, MI: Zondervan Publishing House, 1994), 995.
[xv] R.T. France, *Matthew,* 993.
[xvi] *Matthew,* 994.
[xvii] *Reformed Dogmatics*, Vol. 4., 481ff.
[xviii] Ibid., 483.

CHAPTER SEVEN

The One Another Side of Worship

WORSHIPING HORIZONTALLY

We commonly and rightly emphasize the God-ward dimension when we think about or discuss worship. The Bible places the emphasize here, so we are on safe ground when we do that. However, as we have noted throughout different sections above, worship also has a "one another" side to it or a horizontal dimension that we need to capture as well. The phrase that best captures this side of it is "build up": "When you come together, each one has a hymn, a lesson, a revelation, a tongue, or an interpretation. Let all things be done for building up" (1 Cor. 14:26).

David Peterson has written as forcefully on this issue as anyone, especially because this view challenges common assumptions about the corporate gathering, most notably "designing our gatherings primarily to facilitate private communion with God." He adds,

> *Paul would urge us [in 1 Cor. 14] to meet in dependency on one another as the vehicles of God's grace and to view the well-being and*

> *strengthening of the whole church as the primary aim of the gathering. There ought to be a real engagement with other believers in the context of mutual ministry, shared prayer and praise, not simply a friendly chat over a cup of coffee after church.*[i]

Of course, few things are as edifying for the believer as our "private communion with God," so these aims are not mutually exclusive. Yet, his point is a sound one.

"Build up" comes from the Greek word *oikodomē,* which means "edifying, edification, building up."[ii] The architectural connection is part of the English word as well. We can "build" a building and we can "build up" a friend. Even a building's "edifice" has some relationship to the way I can "edify" another believer.

To make these ideas more concrete, to "build up" another Christian I speak or act in such a way that they become stronger spiritually. That is, their faith is strengthened, their hope is restored, their knowledge of God increases, their desire to please and know God grows, or there is some other similar benefit. When someone comes to a small group meeting discouraged by a relational conflict or another moral failure, my worship leading can build them up by directing their gaze to the sufficiency of Christ and his shed blood that encompasses all of our moral lapses. When someone comes to a Sunday service lonely and despairing, I build them up by drawing the gaze of their hearts to the Christ who says, "I am with you always, to the end of the age" (Matt. 28:20). Such moments bring faith where there is doubt, hope where there is despair, joy where there is depression, peace where there is angst. This is our goal, anyway, even though we won't be able to meet everyone's needs equally in a given time of corporate worship.

Paul uses the term "build up" many times in places like 1 Corinthians 14, which discusses the role of spiritual gifts (vv. 3, 5, 12, 26; cf. also vv. 4, 17), and Ephesians 4, which discusses the role of the offices of the church (vv. 12, 16). Its prominence in these contexts alerts us to its importance in our understanding of corporate worship. But we also find the idea without the word in places like Ephesians 5:19, "addressing one another in psalms and hymns and spiritual songs" (cf. Col. 3:16). Our songs are sung to the Lord, but we also address "one another."

What these passages are getting at is that our worship activities in our church gatherings are not meant only for the Lord. They are also meant for other believers. God is glorified when we biblically worship him, but also as his people are *edified*—built up, encouraged, strengthened, supported in their faith, comforted in their weakness.

In so many ways these concepts are inseparable. God is glorified when his people are edified, and God's people are edified when God is glorified. It is critical that we keep these two ideas together. If we do not, then we run the risk of an overly spiritual understanding of worship (it has nothing to do with us, only God), or we see it as too humanistic (it is simply people helping people grow spiritually). The truth is, the Bible gives us warrant to expect that we can encounter God directly in our corporate meetings. Further, we can please him by our songs and prayers and responses to his revelation. Therefore, the vertical side of our worship must be maintained. We really do relate to God when we gather.

Yet, we also want to remember that worship is not a private moment I am having with the Lord. My brothers and sisters in Christ are with me as we worship. Further, not all of them are doing well. Some of them used all their spiritual vitality just to come through the doors on a Sunday. They actually need me to "build them up" so that they can lift their voices and hearts and hands to the Lord. If I retreat to my private moment with the Lord I may fail them. They might leave without receiving the help they need to worship God. Worship, like all aspects of the Christian life, is a community endeavor. We are God's *people*, not randomly connected persons with no real attachment.

The point of this chapter is to think through several implications of this idea. How does our obligation to build others up affect our corporate worship? That's what we want to consider for the rest of this chapter.

BUILDING OTHERS UP AFFECTS OUR PLANNING

As we have seen, the Bible presents a vast array of worship activities, all of which need to have some place in our services. Yet, there is no precise liturgy provided for us in the Scriptures. How do we plan our gatherings, then? The first step is always to discern the Bible's teaching on the subject. What does it command of us? Once we have wrestled through this issue we recognize that we are presented with a vast list of elements that constitutes "biblical worship." The concept of "building others up" helps me to navigate through this list to plan our service.

We build others up when we remember some basic truths about human weakness. As saints who have yet to be glorified we have limitations in terms of our ability to pay attention. We also have limitations in terms of our time. While the Sunday meeting is certainly the most important block of time in our week, it is not the only one. So, while "more is better" certainly applies to corporate worship, we also need to be aware of the lives people live outside of the Sunday meeting. This applies to visitors as well. They might not understand a church that meets for six hours on a Sunday, thinking it represents extremism, not right Christian zeal. This is not caving into convenience (though we should be on guard for that), but seeing how building others up resonates in our particular cultural context.

We build others when we plan meetings strategically. This means that we make good decisions about what we include and leave out, and also how we transition from one element to another. We want there to be an evident clarity and order to our meetings, and often times that means thinking of simple ways to go from the time of singing to the offering, or from announcements to the sermon, etc. These transitions enable the worshiper to keep up with what we are doing, and also bring to each element expectations that fit the moment.

We also build others up with our planning as we remember certain fixed realities about people. One of these is the power of the Word of God. It alone of all that we do is "breathed out by God" (2 Tim. 3:16) and "truth" that sanctifies (John 17:17). This remains true in every generation in every nation. Thus, it can never be a legitimate decision to leave out the Word of God in a significant way because we feel other elements will edify people more in our setting. This is to cave into the culture, not to lead strategically within our culture.

BUILDING OTHERS UP AFFECTS OUR SONG CHOICES

Another critical area where we can build people up (or not) is in our choice of songs. There are many ways to arrive at our song list for the morning, but keeping our people in mind is essential as we do this. We cannot choose songs simply because they are personal favorites or because we find them personally inspiring. All of us have musical preferences that are forged by what we heard in high school (80s big-hair rock or 90s grunge or hip-hop or Bach), how we have been trained, and our specific church background. Our love of hymns and choirs might mean that we should incorporate more hymns and choirs in our services, or it might just mean that we grew up in a church that had a great choir.

To build others up we take the long view of what our church sings. If we choose only today's worship "top 40" we might be feeding our church the equivalent of Kool-aid and Twinkies. We are leaving out the meat and vegetables that make for a balanced diet. Likewise, if we never sing a song written in this century then we are communicating to our people that God has given our generation no songwriters, no poets, and no musicians of any worth. This is simply not true. Further, in the Psalms we see commands to "sing a new song" (Ps. 33:3; 96:1; 98:1). Each generation has its song to sing of God's redemption and his amazing grace. So, take the long view of choosing songs, incorporating the well-worn paths of classic hymns, but also utilizing quality songs of the present. Such an approach will also help us build churches that are multi-generational. In chapter eleven we'll cover more specific elements of choosing songs for our church.

BUILDING OTHERS UP AFFECTS OUR MUSIC

Our desire to build others up impacts our musical choices. There is no such thing as "the best musical style" for all churches, though there probably is "the best musical style for *our* church." Having a kind of musical center helps people have the right expectations for a given Sunday. It helps us to define ourselves as a church.

Yet, we want to incorporate variety alongside our consistency. No one wants to eat the same food for every meal. Variety helps us to hear the same truths in fresh ways. Further, it provides a small expression of God being worshiped by "all tribes and peoples and languages" (Rev. 7:9). How much variety and what kind of variety to introduce will depend upon our musicians, our congregation, our maturity as a church, our culture, our urban (or rural) setting, and other factors besides.

Strategic variety is yet another way that we can build bridges between cultures and generations. Music is one of the most distinctive aspects of a culture, so incorporating music targeted at a specific age or race can be a powerful way to reach outside of ourselves. Of course, there are dangers with this as well, especially if such attempts are seen as token efforts or insincere or in any way demeaning.

Another side of this is how the lyrics of a song affect how we actually sing it. In general, we can either sing to the Lord or to the congregation. Some songs are third person reflections on the character of God. The hymn, *Here is Love*, examines the cross of Christ and how it beautifully captures the love of God:

Here is love vast as the ocean,
Loving kindness as a flood,
When the Prince of Life, our ransom,
Shed for us His precious blood.[iii]

The perspective of the song is one Christian speaking to another Christian about this marvelous truth. Thus, it would be appropriate to keep our eyes open and think of ourselves as singing this directly to members of our congregation.

In contrast to this, the song, "Thy Mercy, My God," sings directly to the Lord:

Thy mercy, my God,
Is the theme of my song,
The joy of my heart.

And the boast of my tongue.
Thy free grace alone,
From the first to the last,
Hath won my affections,
And bound my soul fast.[iv]

For singing this song it would be entirely appropriate to close our eyes and focus on the Lord himself.

These are only suggestive ideas and by no means absolute laws. We can obviously sing "Thy Mercy, My God" with an emphasis on the congregation and "Here is Love" with a focus on the Lord. These are only examples to show how our desire to build others up might impact how we sing different songs.[v]

BUILDING OTHERS UP AFFECTS SPONTANEITY

Building others up will affect how we utilize spontaneity in our meetings. We might not associate church services with spontaneity, but the Bible does! 1 Corinthians 12-14 reminds us that spiritual gifts bring with them a certain amount of unpredictability, but this spontaneity is to be checked by order, "for God is not a God of confusion but of peace" (1 Cor. 14:33). Further, this spontaneity is not to rob our services of their intelligibility. A visitor to our gatherings should be able to tell what is happening and why—within reason. At the very least, as Paul says, they should not think we are mentally unstable because of what is happening! (1 Cor. 14:23).

On the other side of the spectrum, church is not to resemble a carefully scripted TV show where every part is pre-planned, every set is uniquely designed for this moment, everything is perfectly timed to the second. Such a meeting does not capture the democratic, spiritually vital picture we get from 1 Corinthians 14 (esp. v. 26).

Thus, to build others up we need to lead meetings where spontaneity has a place, but where this spontaneity is guided by discernment and godliness. For some of us this will mean dialing down the unexpected. For others this will mean finding a way to allow for God to break into our carefully laid plans.

An analogy is a basketball team. No quality basketball team has been without a specific game plan that made the best use of its talent and exploited the weaknesses of its opponent. Yet, its success also depended upon its players having the ability to improvise in the moment when opportunities presented themselves. In other words, it was a blend of planning and spontaneity.

One final element to consider here is that we as worship leaders should also see ourselves as those who *facilitate* the spontaneous spiritual gifts of others. Part of our role in corporate worship is to be a means of 1 Corinthians 14:26 actually being fulfilled: "When you come together, each one has a hymn, a lesson, a revelation, a tongue, or an interpretation. Let all things be done for building up." In the corporate worship setting, few people impact how this verse finds expression more than the worship leader. When we function in this way, we are not those who build others up directly, but we are enabling others to perform this critical ministry to their brothers and sisters in Christ.[vi]

BUILDING OTHERS UP AFFECTS OUR EVALUATION

Finally, building others up also affects how we evaluate our services. We can use dozens of different approaches to answer the question, 'Was our service effective?', but one of the key ones has to be, 'Were people built up?' That is, were people strengthened, challenged, supported, and comforted in their faith? Did they leave more aware of God's power than their weakness, more aware of his forgiveness than their sin, more aware of the truth of his word than the doubt in their hearts? Did they find God wherever they were in their spiritual journey?

These are difficult questions to answer, and we want to be careful about claiming omniscience here. What worship leader has not had the experience of being ready to leave the stage and go straight to the senior pastor to resign from *ever* doing this again, only to hear from many people how blessed they were by the songs and the words he said? Sometimes God crafts situations for the express purpose of reminding us that *it's not about us, it's about him*. With that caveat, we do want to try and get a general read on how people were affected today, and how they are being affected week in, week out by the services that we are holding.

One thing to note here is that this is a much more biblical and encouraging way to assess a meeting than more superficial gauges like attendance or the size of the offering. At some point attendance and the offering are affected by the spiritual vitality of a service, but these are really symptoms of an issue, not its cause. A question like whether people are being edified or not gets at deeper and ultimately more important areas to address.

To get at the answer to this question we might note how many people come to the prophecy microphone, how energetically the congregation was responding to our direction, how enthusiastically they were singing the songs, how many spontaneous "Amen's!" came from the audience, how many hands were raised during certain songs, how engaged we ourselves were during the singing, etc. A general truth to grasp is that when someone is edified on the inside, it will be evident on the outside. Just like joy and sadness on the inside always find their way out, so does being built up in our faith—or not.

IT'S STILL ABOUT HIM

Our emphasis on building up other believers (and unbelievers) does not change the fact that worship is ultimately about God. Paul said that "whether you eat or drink, or whatever you do, do all to the glory of God" (1 Cor. 10:31). If this is true of food and drink, how much more true is it of worship services? Peter summarized the purpose for being "a chosen race, a royal priesthood, a holy nation" by saying that we are to "proclaim the excellencies of him who called you out of darkness into his marvelous light" (1 Peter 2:9).

Our only point in this chapter is that the goal of bringing glory to God is to be joined to our goal of building up the body of Christ. Thus, our songs are aimed at God to please him, and at our brothers and sisters in Christ to strengthen them; our prayers are first directed to the God who answers prayer, and then toward those who are hearing us pray to him. Let us work for the glory of God while we also work toward the good of our brothers and sisters.

NOTES

[i] *Engaging with God* (Downers Grove, IL: InterVarsity Press, 1992), 214.

[ii] *A Greek-English Lexicon of the New Testament and Other Early Christian Literature*, eds. Danker, Ardnt, Gingrich, Bauer (Chicago, IL: The University of Chicago Press, 2000).

[iii] "Here is Love," lyrics by William Rees (1802-1883). Public domain.

[iv] "Thy Mercy, My God," lyrics by John Stocker. Public domain.

[v] Bob Kauflin inspired this idea and Philip Sasser reminded me of the concept in discussions on this chapter.

[vi] Brad Hodges contributed this insight.

PART THREE

Leading Worship

CHAPTER EIGHT

Juggling Flaming Torches Overview of the Worship Leading Task

ONE JUGGLER TO ANOTHER

A New York Times article from March 15, 1988, described the Ridge Street School in Manhattan. Dan Markowitz said

> *There are tens of thousands of three-ball juggling tricks, Ms. King said, and new tricks are invented every day. Some of the most popular are the yo-yo and the oy-oy, Mill's Mess, Rubenstein's Revenge and the box. Besides balls, clubs, bean bags and fruit, rings, scarves and even bowling balls are commonly juggled. Machetes and lit torches, props often used by performance jugglers, are not allowed at the Rye Brook club. Juggling while riding a unicycle, plate spinning and a device called the diablo are also part of the juggler's routine.*
>
> *Michael totes a gym bag stuffed with his juggling paraphernalia.*
>
> *"'There's tremendous variation," Mr. Howard said. "Boring it's never."*

> *Mr. Davis, a playwright who spends two to three hours a day practicing juggling, said: "Once you get to a certain technical level, it's all hard. The point for me is to make it look as easy as possible."*
>
> *But there's no perfection, Ms. King said. "Anytime you think you have it mastered, just add one more object and you're back where you started."*[i]

Over the years I have compared worship leading more to juggling than anything else. To say, "tremendous variation," is an understatement." To say, "boring it's never," is entirely true. And after years of doing it, I can attest that "anytime you think you have it mastered, just add one more object and you're back where you started."

When I went from leading with only a guitar to leading with a band, I added a couple more balls to keep in the air. When I went from college students to a mixed congregation, I added a couple more. When I went from loving the music and the mood to wanting to be thoroughly biblical in my practice and theology of worship, I added another one.

The truth is, every time I added more balls to keep in the air, I spent months or years leaving at least a few on the floor after a time of worship. I would focus on experiencing God and leave the ball on the floor labeled "the Lord's Supper." I would try and keep Scripture reading in our times of worship and leave the ball on the floor labeled "spontaneous experience of the Holy Spirit."

But, there's more. We are not simply juggling bean bags. It is more like the "machetes and lit torches" they outlaw at the juggling school. Our "plate spinning" is not plastic-ware, but fine china. Why do I say that? Because when you drop a bean bag or grab one wrong, no one gets hurt and there is no mess. But, when you drop a flaming torch or grab it wrong....Ouch. I wish I could say my track record of leading worship was without incident, but the truth is, small fires and shattered glass just about sums up any number of Sunday mornings or small group times of worship leading. Sundays can feel like an impossible act of juggling.

In the chapters ahead we will look at several aspects that we are "juggling." This chapter will start with something more basic, more fundamental, because our juggling metaphor breaks down if it makes us into entertainers or somehow *the most important person in the room*. In other words, we need to get a clear sense of what we *are*, before we can look at what we *do*.

There are six ways we need to think of ourselves in this role as worship leader: a means of grace, a man of character, a man under authority, a servant, a worshiper, and a leader. The order is important for too often we start with our place as a "leader" of corporate worship, and it becomes all about the tasks we perform on any given Sunday. Our long-term effectiveness has everything to do with how we view ourselves in the larger context of the body of Christ.

A MEANS OF GRACE

First, a worship leader is a means of grace. A "means" is something necessary to accomplish something, but not the essential thing. When the UPS man delivers a package to my house he is a "means" to get the package from one place to another, but the important thing is the package. His importance has to do with the importance of the package he's carrying. To be a means *of grace* is to be a way that God transmits his grace to people. That is a glorious and humbling role to fill, but the critical element is the *grace* that gets passed from God to people. All that we do is meant to help people receive the grace of God.

"Grace" is a catch-all term for whatever is needed by a person in the moment. Sometimes people need power to obey, sometimes it's forgiveness for sins, sometimes it's hope for discouragement, sometimes it's wisdom for a decision. The way that God meets us in our time of need we are calling "grace" here.

Being a "means" of grace is being the human agent God uses to accomplish his work in people. When a preacher communicates God's truth powerfully, he is simply the human means God is using. He could have used other means, like a donkey (Num. 22:21-30), but typically it is people like you and me. Thus, humanly speaking, worship leading begins with the worship leader, and a fruitful worship ministry within a church likewise involves the man who oversees that ministry. We see the principle from beginning to end in our Bible that God always uses a human agent to accomplish his purposes in a group of people. Corporate worship is no exception.

Often our problem is overstating our importance in the process. A sign that we are losing sight of our place versus God's place is the overwhelming anxiety we can feel at times, usually derived from a false sense that everything depends upon us. At that point we are forgetting that whatever we do, we do by grace through faith empowered by his Spirit. The beginning of the chain is grace and every link along the way is grace. So while it is true that we must work hard (Rom. 12:8), the chief part of that work is to trust that all depends on the Lord. Anxiety is the tipoff that we have forgotten this and are living in the lie that my efforts are the decisive ones.

So, anxiety gets us on one side, but pride can get us on the other. Pride snags us when we assume that we are irreplaceable. We assume that our worship leading (with all of its strengths and weaknesses, influences, idiosyncrasies, etc.) is the only solution for this local church. Yes, we are uniquely gifted and created by God, but we are also replaceable. This is not to make us indifferent, but humble. God has gifted and chosen you for this season of your church and we are to be faithful as long as this remains true. We must remember that another will likely replace us. Chances are good that a lot of what we changed they will also change, and they will be fruitful in ways we never could be. Truly, anxiety and pride are indicators that we are thinking wrongly about our place in the worship of our church.

So remember, as a worship leader you are a *means of grace*. The grace is the critical thing and the grace is all God's. We are the means that God uses to deliver it to others.

A MAN OF CHARACTER

Second, a worship leader must be a man of character—not perfection, but character. Paul addresses Timothy with words which have great application for the worship leader as well: "Keep a close watch on yourself and on the teaching" (1 Tim. 4:16). This speaks first to our integrity. We get a beautiful and challenging picture of our integrity in 1 Timothy 3:8-13 where Paul speaks of the character required of deacons. The worship leader may be an elder or a commissioned deacon, but even if he is not, he should at least be deacon-like in his character. This is because he has such a visible role, and he bears significant spiritual responsibility in the corporate service.[ii] Thus, what kind of men are we to be? This kind of man:

> *Deacons likewise must be dignified, not double-tongued, not addicted to much wine, not greedy for dishonest gain.*
> *9 They must hold the mystery of the faith with a clear conscience.*
> *10 And let them also be tested first; then let them serve as deacons if they prove themselves blameless.*
> *11 Their wives likewise must be dignified, not slanderers, but sober-minded, faithful in all things.*
> *12 Let deacons each be the husband of one wife, managing their children and their own households well.*
> *13 For those who serve well as deacons gain a good standing for themselves and also great confidence in the faith that is in Christ Jesus. (1 Tim. 3:8-13)*

This passage paints the picture of a godly and authentic man, one whose life demonstrates a basic self-control, whose faith is legitimate and growing, whose wife models biblical womanhood, and whose home shows the marks of his effective leadership. Such qualifications are intimidating and humbling, but we should trust God that he will raise up men like this to lead us in worship. Being a man of gifting and a man of integrity—that is what it should mean to be a worship leader in your church.

To "keep a close watch on yourself" (1 Tim. 4:16) also speaks to our relationship with the Lord. Just as Jesus himself withdrew to fellowship with the Father, so we should make this a routine practice (Mark 6:46). We are not self-sufficient. We need the Lord. We need his grace. We need his Word. We need his

Spirit. Let us go to the place where we find him—in his Word and prayer.

Since we are serving as worship leaders we should also take care that we are growing in our understanding of worship and the depth of our personal worship. We might not be as flamboyant as we were ten years ago, but let us be more in love with God and better worshipers of God than we were then!

A MAN UNDER AUTHORITY

Third, a worship leader is to be a man under authority. In some churches the primary worship leader will be a member of the pastoral team, but for many churches this is not the case. Here, as in all aspects of church life, we must recognize the place of God's chosen authority, the elders. The author of Hebrews commands us, "Obey your leaders and submit to them, for they are keeping watch over your souls, as those who will have to give an account. Let them do this with joy and not with groaning, for that would be of no advantage to you" (13:17). While our effectiveness as worship *leaders* requires us to step out boldly as we sense the Lord leading us, it also requires us to joyfully submit to the Lord's leadership through the elders. They must define for us the goals, length, style, and various roles of our corporate worship. In fact, one of the critical tests for whether we are hearing the Lord's guidance is how the elders respond to it.

In a healthy situation there is plenty of back-and-forth between the worship leader and the elders. Sometimes it's the elders giving specific direction to the worship leader, but sometimes the worship leader is offering suggestions (or challenges) about a new direction for the church's corporate worship. A worship leader should trust that God will bring great blessing as he submits to the elders, and that the worship of that church will thrive as he works within the boundaries established by the leaders God has called to pastor his church.

A SERVANT

Fourth, a worship leader must be a servant. Jesus said that "whoever would be first among you must be slave of all" (Mark

10:44). As a "slave" (Grk., *doulos)* we have no rights, no ability to govern ourselves. We serve at the pleasure of the Master, and we walk as he directs. To walk as a servant "of all" does not mean that everyone else is our master and we do whatever anyone tells us to do. It means that we devote our energy and resources to blessing others. Christ remains our true and only Master (Rom. 14:4), but under his lordship we give ourselves to benefit others.

This role as servants of the church does not change when we become leaders of some aspect of church life. It only changes the nature of my service. As a father I serve my family by leading my family, and as a worship leader I serve my church by leading them in their corporate worship. If I try and lead without also knowing I am a servant, I run the risk of being a tyrant, self-willed, have an inflated view of myself, and take the people places that do not bless them.

Being a servant means I need to know the people I lead. Proverbs 27:23 says to "know well the condition of your flocks, and give attention to your herds." This nugget holds true in worship leading as well. I need to lead with a knowledge of those I am leading—their experience, their preferences, their history, their spiritual maturity, their past worship experiences. I need to understand their lives—what have they experienced this week, this year? I need to recall the current Sunday preaching. Even the calendar has some impact—holidays at times, the New Year, major world events, etc. In our role we are shepherds trying to bring the people to some place other than where they are. They might come as employees, fathers, and housewives, but we are trying to give them a fresh awareness that they are above all worshipers of an all-glorious God.

Our role as servants affects many of the practicals of our corporate worship: song choices, arrangements, length of worship, volume, the sound system, the room, featured instruments, the default sound of the team, etc. All of these issues can be an act of self-promotion or basic selfishness ("We're doing this sound because *I like it*"), or an act of service ("For the sake of helping bring these people into a greater awareness of God, let's integrate more musical styles in our sets").

Being a servant impacts how we approach creativity. Generally, people are served if creativity is incorporated into a basic consistency. Another way to say it is that creativity serves people, but unpredictability does not. Of course, consistency can drift toward monotony, and neither does that serve people.

Thus, as a worship leader, let your ideas, initiative, energy, bold and spontaneous leadership, and overall vision be flavored by your heart to serve your people.

A WORSHIPER

Fifth, a worship leader is to be a worshiper. This might seem like an obvious one, but the flurry of details that come together for corporate worship can sometimes make this extremely difficult. At such times we feel more like a *juggler* than a worshiper, but we ought never forget that before we are a *worship leader* we are simply a worshiper. There is a task we are called to do that demands focus and energy, but we must regularly go back to the truth that I am a child of God who delights in his heavenly Father and who enjoys worshiping his great name. We are not performers. We are not first musicians. Above all these things we are worshipers. Without question this is brutally difficult. But, it is essential.

One aspect of this is being intentional to think about the words that we sing.[iii] Its simplicity might deceive us into missing the usefulness of the insight, but truly if we can discipline our minds to mean what we sing and to sing what we mean, then we will go a long way toward worshiping while we lead.

Another aspect of worship leading being worship is that it is part of a whole life of worship. Just as being a good bus driver means not closing my eyes and losing myself in biblical meditation, so there are times when I surrender some of my private worship for the sake of a larger purpose. This is not a problem since our whole lives are worship offered to God: "I appeal to you therefore, brothers, by the mercies of God, to present your bodies as a living sacrifice, holy and acceptable to God, which is your spiritual worship" (Rom. 12:1).

A LEADER

Sixth, a worship leader is also a leader. We have deliberately placed this last so that we could get a more accurate picture of the leadership we are to provide. It is a leadership that serves, that comes from the heart of a worshipper submitted to the authorities God has given to his church, that sees its role in helping people receive the grace of God. But, once we have grasped some of these qualifiers we are indeed to be courageous leaders. There are three ways that leadership is needed from us.

1. Leadership involves providing a compelling and biblical vision for the worship ministry of the church. The first priority of our leadership, assuming we are leading the overall worship ministry of the church, is to provide the worship team with a compelling and biblical vision for corporate worship. This does not happen in a single teaching or a few months of emphasis. It is built over years and reinforced in subtle and emphatic ways throughout team meetings, articles and books read, conferences attended, conversations had, calls to worship given, and corporate worship experienced. At its core such a vision should think through what we are doing and why we are doing it and for whom we are doing it. All of this must of course be derived from the word of God, though we will inevitably be inspired by other teachers and books.

How our vision is communicated will depend upon our place in the overall worship of the church. It might be that we build these convictions only in the worship team and through our calls to worship. Perhaps we will occasionally teach the whole church about biblical worship. Regardless of where we get to share our vision, the first step is to establish a set of biblical convictions on worship. A patient and lengthy study on the topic will be the only way to do this. Yet, this is part of the leadership required of us.

2. Leadership involves building a worship team that is growing spiritually, musically, and relationally. Second, leadership must be directed at building the team itself. The men and women who give their time and talents to serve the church are likely gifted, committed people. Yet, all of us need to be growing to be fully engaged in what we are doing. Further, the importance of the task itself requires us to give our best to see that it is done as well as we can possibly do it.

The leader should consider how to help his people to grow spiritually, which means growing in their relationship with Jesus Christ and their knowledge of God himself. Maybe this is more about making sure that people are doing well overall, walking in faith and pursuing God in their personal devotions, etc.

We will naturally think about helping people to grow musically, because the task itself drives us to do that. Doing this strategically and consistently is more challenging, but part of our leadership is keeping before the team a musical vision of what you are striving to attain.

The leader must also be concerned that the team is actually *a team*, a group that is growing relationally in addition to these other areas. Sometimes a cookout and hanging out will accomplish more than yet another teaching.

This team-focused side of our leadership means also that the worship leader needs to watch over his team like a shepherd watching over his sheep. We want to make sure people are well served by being on the team. Their spiritual health is more important than our musical goals. We want to make it easy for someone to take time off if they need to and to find a warm reception when they return.

3. Leadership involves leading…the corporate worship. The third broad area of our leadership is the one we most naturally think of when it comes to being a worship leader, namely, leading corporate worship. In chapter eleven we will look at more practical dimensions of leading this part of our meetings, but here we can underscore that leadership *is* required. Even though we gather as "the body of Christ" with all of us being only a part (Rom. 12:4-5), and though we want to build the expectation that everyone will come with some contribution (1 Cor. 14:26), leadership is required to see that all of this happens. A large meeting without leadership is rarely a 'beautiful display of the spontaneous work of the Spirit,' but more often resembles one raucous crowd described in the Bible: "Now some cried out one thing, some another, for the assembly was in confusion, and most of them did not know why they had come together" (Acts 19:32). More directly we can look at 1 Corinthians 14:33 and see that while we should promote and defend spiritual gifts, we should do this with the understanding that "God is not a God of confusion but of peace." Leadership helps us to protect both the gifts of the Spirit and the picture of our God of peace.

CONCLUSION: JUST ONE

It's possible that what I've shared in this chapter feels like I just threw six more flaming torches at you, and you feel a tad off-balance. Here it is good to employ some advice I heard first from David Powlison about application. Most of us can only deal with one new emphasis or practice at a time. Take the six topics we covered in this chapter and choose just one to be an emphasis for a period of time. Later you can add another one. Likely, however, some of these are more natural for you than others. Maybe choose one that is more of a challenge and prayerfully consider how you can grow with that side of being a worship leader. And because we so easily lose sight of it, remember, worship is about God, not us.

NOTES

[i] Dan Markowitz, "Where Jugglers of All Ages Practice," obtained at http://www.nytimes.com/1998/03/15/nyregion/where-jugglers-of-all-ages-practice.html on March 17, 2011.

[ii] There are obviously differences of opinion on this subject. Some do not see the role as diaconal and they reduce the character requirement of the man (or woman in some churches). Our own conviction on this subject is that the amount and visibility of his responsibility makes the role at least deacon-like. Further, people assume that key leaders on the stage on Sundays—teachers of God's Word, those who give announcements, worship leaders, etc.—are examples of godliness as the church understands that. Thus, a man who has such a platform ministry should be a man the elders consider a worthy example of godliness for the church to emulate—not perfect, but godly.

[iii] On this point I am indebted to Bob Kauflin who has written on this and spoken on this in a variety of contexts. Cf. www.worshipmatters.com;

Worship Matters (Wheaton, IL: Crossway Books, 2008); the Worship God conferences that he leads (www.sovereigngraceministries.org/).

CHAPTER NINE

Calls to Worship

In this chapter we turn to what is often labeled the "call to worship." While we have our own history vis-à-vis this practice, it is an element with a long history in the church and cuts across all denominational lines. It is also a responsibility that rests uniquely on the worship leader. That is why we have placed it in Part Three as opposed to Part Four of this book.

Bryan Chapell provides a useful definition of the "call to worship" that paints a good picture of this part of our service:

> *In the historical practice of Christian churches across many traditions, a Call to Worship typically is a few lines of Scripture (or a combination of Scripture texts) expressed by a minister or worship leader at the beginning of a church service. In contemporary practice, a Call to Worship may be extemporized by the worship leader, presented by a choir, read responsively by the congregation, sung by a worship team, or included in an opening song, but the goal does not vary for those who understand the significance of these moments. The Call to Worship exhorts God's people to turn from worldly distractions*

and to focus hearts, minds, and actions on revering him.[i]

For many churches Chapell's description fits perfectly. The "few lines of Scripture" might be a well-chosen portion of a Psalm like 146:1-2:

Praise the LORD!
Praise the LORD, O my soul!
[2] *I will praise the LORD as long as I live;*
I will sing praises to my God
while I have my being. (Ps. 146:1-2)

In our tradition the call to worship is given by the worship leader, generally after an opening song. Our goals mirror Chapell's closely: "exhorts God's people to turn from worldly distractions and to focus hearts, minds, and actions on revering him." In fact, we have often termed this call to worship, "the exhortation," because that is the dominant voice of these moments in our service.

For the sake of our discussion we will define the call to worship this way:

The call to worship is a brief segment of our service guided by or spoken by the worship leader, which is intended to provoke the people of God to worship the Lord. It will typically consist of a clear truth and a call to an appropriate response. It might include such things as a Scripture text or quote with comments, a responsive reading, or even a carefully worded prayer.

This "brief segment" may last anywhere from one to three minutes or so and most often consists of the worship leader reading a portion of Scripture and then calling the church to respond in worship. Thus, truth is joined to a call for response. What we choose to do for the call to worship—Scripture text, quote, responsive reading, etc.—is very flexible. The basic goal of this element is less so.

Of the many flaming torches we are juggling, this is one I have dropped on numerous occasions. Sometimes it is being entirely incoherent. Sometimes it is reading passages of Scripture or a book far too long for this moment of the service. Sometimes it is calling people to a response without really preparing them for it. The word "alone" comes to mind. Sometimes it is something as basic as talking too fast to be heard or mumbling into the microphone. Sometimes it is not working hard enough to communicate a familiar truth in a fresh way. The torch drops and then our task becomes rebuilding some lost momentum and doing damage control. Hopefully this section will help us to avoid some of these drops.

THE BIBLICAL MANDATE FOR CALLS TO WORSHIP

While it might seem fairly obvious that calling the people of God to worship God is well within the basic mission of the church, it is still useful to see how often the Bible engages us in calls to worship. Here are four examples from different sections of our Bibles that serve as vivid models for us:

> *"Stand up and bless the LORD your God from everlasting to everlasting. Blessed be your glorious name, which is exalted above all blessing and praise." (Neh. 9:5)*

> *Oh come, let us sing to the LORD;*
> *let us make a joyful noise*
> *to the rock of our salvation!*
> 2 *Let us come into his presence*
> *with thanksgiving;*
> *let us make a joyful noise to him*
> *with songs of praise!*
> 3 *For the LORD is a great God,*
> *and a great King above all gods.*
> *(Ps. 95:1-3)*

> *I appeal to you therefore, brothers, by the mercies of God, to present your bodies as a living sacrifice, holy and acceptable to God, which is your spiritual worship. (Rom. 12:1)*

> *But you are a chosen race, a royal priesthood, a holy nation, a people for his own possession, that you may proclaim the excellencies of him who called you out of darkness into his marvelous light. [10] Once you were not a people, but now you are God's people; once you had not received mercy, but now you have received mercy. (1 Peter 2:9-10)*

The call to worship in Nehemiah 9:5 is emphatic and leans more into the response required ("Stand up and bless the LORD") than into a reason for doing this. Why we are to do this is given as the actual prayer unfolds: "You are the LORD, you alone," etc. (v. 6).

The Psalm 95:1-3 example is written from the perspective of the worship leader calling others to join him in praising God: "Oh come, let us sing to the LORD." It begins with the responses called for—"sing…make a joyful noise…thanksgiving…joyful noise…songs of praise"—and then provides a clear reason to exalt our God in this way: "For the LORD is a great God, and a great king above all gods" (v. 3).

Romans 12:1 "appeals" for God's people to see the great mercy of the gospel unpacked in Romans 1-11 ("therefore"), and then to worship "by the mercies of God." Worship is seen as presenting "your bodies as a living sacrifice, holy and acceptable to God, which is your spiritual worship." The truth presented is "the mercies of God," and the response requested is to present our bodies as living sacrifices.

1 Peter 2:9-10 approaches the call to worship slightly differently. Peter expresses worship as the great purpose for God's redemptive work in his people. We became a new people "that you may proclaim the excellencies of him who called you out of

darkness into his marvelous light." We "received mercy" through the gospel, and this was so that we might worship him.

These are a few of many examples throughout the Bible that model what we are wanting to emulate: relatively brief, compelling calls for the people of God to offer themselves in sincere worship to their glorious God. The way that they combine a clear truth and a call for response is something we will explore further below.

Such texts also remind us that whatever else our call to worship is, it must be biblical. We will not help people if we motivate them with something that fails this basic test. There are obvious ways to make a mistake here: "Let's give praise to the Father for dying on the cross for our sins." All of us have either said things like this or heard them said. Most of the time it is misspeaking something we understand clearly and is attributable to nerves. Sometimes, however, it is an actual misunderstanding that we need to correct.

Other areas are more subtle: "Let's enter into his presence now with thanksgiving in our hearts." We might be paraphrasing Psalm 100:4, but we are also being unclear. Since Christ has opened the way to the Father through offering his own blood we do not "enter into his presence" in this way. It has already been accomplished. In this more subtle way we have failed the test of being biblical. *Being biblical is the highest priority for the person who has a public role in the corporate worship of the church.*

THREE BROAD CATEGORIES OF THE CALL TO WORSHIP

We said above that calls to worship should combine a clear statement of truth with a call for a response of worship. There are three basic categories of calls to worship that approach this task differently. The first two (Explanatory, Doxological) lean into the truth that we present. The third (Exhortational) leans into the response that the church gives.

1. The Explanatory Call to Worship: "This is Why...." The first category is a "*This is why...*" call to worship. That is, we might explain why a certain practice like singing or raising our hands or clapping or prophecy should have a place in our corporate worship. We might explain that worship is something we have been doing all week privately, and now we experience the joy of doing it corporately. We might explain what our service will look like for visitors. There are any number of possibilities, all of which help inspire faith in those who will do these practices.

The benefit of such an exhortation is that people's understanding of the corporate worship of the church is increased over time. This can be an excellent way to teach God's people in small and regular ways.

To do this we might go to 1 Corinthians 14:1 which says, "Pursue love, and earnestly desire the spiritual gifts, especially that you may prophesy." Why? Because "the one who prophesies speaks to people for their upbuilding and encouragement and consolation" (v. 3). We can read and explain such a text and maybe point out the way someone might do this in our meeting.

One thing to remember with such exhortations is that they tend to place the focus on ourselves. It can be helpful to redirect our attention back to the Lord after we have given the explanation. We might explain prophecy but add, "And what is so amazing about prophecy? God wants to speak to us! He is here! He knows what we are experiencing and wants to speak into our situations!"

2. The Doxological Call to Worship: "God is…." This is the "God is…" kind of call to worship. Here we are highlighting something of God's attributes, ways, purposes, plans, or works. These are not truths for information's sake, but springboards to worship. We can think here of the numerous times in the Psalms that we see the command, "Give thanks to the LORD, for he is good" (e.g., 136:1). This is a simple way of highlighting a truth about God ("he is good"), but calling us to respond to it ("Give thanks to the LORD"). What makes it a *doxological* call to worship as opposed to the *explanatory* call to worship is that most of our time will be spent in highlighting the attributes or works of God. It will be at the end when we provide a brief call to respond: "Since God is this way, let's lift up our hearts and voices to him!"

3. The Exhortational Call to Worship: "Worship God by...." This category of the call to worship leans into the response of the congregation, some version of "Worship God by _____!" For example, *"Worship God by raising your hands, or lifting your voices, or clapping, or dancing, etc.!"* This is a more direct exhortation, urging people to *do* something immediately. We might urge people to trust God, believe in him, rely on him, run to him, draw near to him; or practical actions like singing, raising our hands, or shouting our praises to him. The opening of Psalm 47 is an example of this: "Clap your hands, all peoples! Shout to God with loud songs of joy!" (v. 1). The content might be similar to the *explanatory call to worship* above, but the mood and language will be quite different.

These categories are somewhat arbitrary, but they do point us toward the basic intent for these exhortations or calls to worship. In all of them we are wanting to highlight a specific truth and our worshipful response to that truth. Sometimes we are more aware of the truth and sometimes more aware of the response, but both should be present. In this we are echoing the thoughts of Bryan Chapell:

> *A Call to Worship has an imperative quality. We are not simply informing others of the attributes of God or creating a holy aura by the citation of a poignant Scripture passage. In the Call to Worship, the worship leader specifically calls God's people to respond to God's revelation.*[ii]

3 C'S OF EFFECTIVE CALLS TO WORSHIP

Like anything done publicly there are ways to do it that are more effective and less effective. Here are three things to consider as we craft our calls to worship.

1. The call to worship should be clear. First, because exhortations tend to be very short—usually three or four minutes—they must be extremely clear. This means that they need to be monothematic, having a single theme. There is not time to develop more than one idea, and there is little time to do even one.

Thus, we cannot develop a truth to a great extent in addition to the appropriate response. We must choose to accent the truth *or* the response.

This brevity also requires that our exhortations be immediately accessible to be clear. They have to be as obvious as a TV commercial or a bumper sticker—though massively more significant. There is not time to explain a complex idea or use multiple Scripture references to make a point. Such immediate accessibility affects our words and sentences and vocabulary. No one is reading what we are saying and cannot re-read a complex thought. Thus, we are using a "spoken style" in our call to worship, not a "written style." Even if we write out our calls to worship we need to remember this.

Clarity also relates to how well our call to worship fits the overall flow of the service. Our songs should support our call to worship, and our call to worship should support our songs. As Chapell says, "A well-planned Call to Worship often reflects the theme of the service or the nature of the occasion so that the remaining elements of the service are a natural outflow of, and response to, the content or the call."[iii]

2. The call to worship should be concise. Second, our calls to worship should be concise. People know the difference between the sermon and the corporate praise time. They get nervous when they think you do not! Our goal is to provide a true reason for the people of God to respond in sincere worship. Other contexts need to be used to build our larger theology of worship (sermons, books, etc.). If we go too long we lose momentum, and people begin to drift in their minds.

This can happen when our thoughts are too wordy, and it can even happen with our use of Scripture. The efficient use of Scripture is critical. There is a place for longer Scripture readings or longer responsive readings, but we must be intentional as we do this. Too often our real burden is a two to three verse passage, and yet we end up reading the entire ten or twenty verses of the paragraph or Psalm. Providing a context is commendable, but it often dilutes the impact of the reading. People are not as familiar with the text as you are and are working hard to keep up. This extra effort means they are less able to respond to the key part of the passage that you wanted to convey. The Psalms can be particularly tricky because they often deal with a variety of themes in a variety of ways. The basic idea here is to read only enough to convey the burden from the text (again, unless the point is to read a longer passage, in which case we need to set it up and read it particularly well).

This is not a statement that modern man cannot handle the "public reading of Scripture" (1 Tim. 4:13), an explicit command of Scripture. Or that we need to cave in because of average attention spans. It is merely an appeal to be intentional. If you want to read a long passage, prepare the congregation. If you believe your church needs to add the reading of entire chapters to its worship, then be intentional. Explain what you are doing and why. Help them to build the same conviction that you have. With that caveat said, be concise.

3. The call to worship should be compelling. Anything that we do publicly with the gathered people of God becomes a significant opportunity to see God work. For that reason we always want to feel the burden to be compelling. To be compelling in a call to worship means that the people of God are provoked to worship God as a response to what we say.

In presenting truth we are compelling if we present familiar truths and ideas in fresh ways. We are by no means changing the truth itself. Instead we are working to affect hearts and minds with truths that we know well. The truth that "Christ died for our sins" (1 Cor. 15:3) is a matter "of first importance," but it might not affect us in this way if we do not work to creatively communicate this truth.

Being compelling also requires that we connect such truth to a specific response. We are not presenting truth for its own sake—the Bible never does this. The truth we present is meant to provoke a response of worship. If we too often drift toward presenting truth without a call for response, then we can create the "fat heads—dead hearts" or "dead orthodoxy" style of worship. Likewise, if we too often call for response without giving clear truth, then we run the risk of emotionalism and building a lot of energy without real rootedness in the truth of God.

One aspect of this is that the more you lead in a given context the harder you will have to work. If you lead a group of people in worship only one time your presence there is enough newness to affect them afresh. Yet, if you stand in front of your church 30-50 times per year as the main leader, you will need to work much harder to be compelling.

This cuts both ways. You have to work harder to come up with 30-50 distinct thoughts and worship sets than to produce one. And for your congregation they will be more tempted to distraction the more familiar they are with you. Creativity is a way that we serve our people and work to inspire their worship of God.

Such creativity does not need to be overdone to be effective. We do not need dynamic multi-media presentations to wow our congregations for the sake of creativity. That can actually hinder sincere worship when they return to the "same old singing with the same old band." Of course, something elaborate done occasionally can be an effective tool.

More typical creative elements might be varying slightly what you do. We can freshly affect people by adding responsive readings, dramatic readings, special music, adding Scriptures throughout a known hymn, or any number of things. We also serve people by being mindful of the themes that we address and the songs that we use. Sometimes when we are not intentional about such things we can default to the same half-dozen or dozen themes/Scriptures because "they always worked before."

One caution when it comes to such matters is to remember the point. Creativity makes a wonderful servant but a terrible master. Creativity is being utilized in these cases to serve a higher call: *we want God's truth to affect people at a deep level.* Our goal is not creativity that earns the respect of an unbelieving culture. Our goal is presenting God's truth in a way that inspires sincere worship. Creativity can be a wonderful means in accomplishing such a goal.

A final aspect of being compelling is knowing when to include "I's" and when to stick with "We's," a point expressed to me recently by Joe Jackson, the worship leader at Redeeming

Grace Church (Durham, NC). The call to worship is a place where we want to be authentic with people. We are not disinterested parties presenting objective truth that doesn't resonate in our souls. Imagine the mechanic who looks at your car to see if it passed its annual inspection. You don't expect him to be emotional as he says your car, unfortunately, has emissions too great for the government's standard. He'll just deliver the information and let you know what to do about it.

A call to worship is different because we are inviting God's people to join us in something that we ourselves are eager to do. This means that we can and should speak with "I's" at times. We might share how God met us personally. We might reveal where we were tempted not to believe the truth we are sharing. Sometimes we are experiencing something that most (or all) of the church knows about. Especially at those times it can be appropriate to share about what "I received from the Lord."

Speaking with "We's" has to do with more general truth that is always relevant for the people of God. People might enter into it very personally, but it is basically a general truth that "We should remember as we sing to the Lord."

The man I've seen best do this is Joe Jackson, now the worship leader at Redeeming Grace Church (Durham, NC). His skill at doing this comes from keeping the central point central. The point is not what we experienced or felt, but what God did or showed to us. We don't need to hear a five or ten-minute story to get the gist of the situation. People need some basic details to understand where you are coming from, but the bulk of the time needs to be spent on the truth about God we want people to take away. Joe is able to draw us into his situation briefly, but then call us to look upward and outward at the grace available to us in Christ.

As with most things in our calls to worship, we can get in trouble if we speak in only one way—always "We's" or never "We's." The trick is the right balance for us personally and for the context in which we lead.

Thus, there are many ways to get at giving a compelling call to worship. Each person will be better at some ways than others, and each of us needs to find how we best do it. We need to find our voice, as it were, and tap into that way of speaking. It can take real effort, but the effort will bear much fruit in our corporate worship times.

GETTING PRACTICAL

To make this as practical as possible, here is a simple approach to create a call to worship. *First, choose your text.* Pick a text of a reasonable length (2-5 verses) that has a truth you and your people need to hear. You do not need to feel the pressure of choosing 'the perfect text.' All of them are "breathed out by God" (2 Tim. 3:16).

Second, meditate on the text. Pray over it. Say it over and over. Write out your observations about the text. What is the text saying? What are the key points made? How does it want us to respond? Restate the burden of the text in your own words. It is a helpful goal to get to the point where you can summarize the burden of the text in a single phrase or sentence.

Third, sketch out a call to worship. Think in terms of a beginning, the main point, and a transition. In the beginning you are addressing your people for perhaps the first time. How do you want to start? For the main point, how will you develop the main burden of the call to worship? Simple, clear, concise, easy sentences and vocabulary, good energy in your delivery and language—these are some things to keep in mind. For the end, think of a final 1-2 sentences that take the group from the call to worship to the next song.

WORTH THE EFFORT

Without question, giving effective calls to worship requires work. Yet, the benefits of this labor are manifold. First, our own soul is edified as we wrestle with God's truth and how we can present it to his people. Second, there is the benefit that our congregation receives as they are given foundational truths in a way that affects them. Third and most important, we are proving faithful to our Savior and Lord. His pleasure is the greatest benefit his servants can receive.

NOTES

[i] *Christ-Centered Worship: Letting the Gospel Shape our Practice* (Baker Academic: Grand Rapids, MI, 2009), 159.

[ii] Ibid., 161.

[iii] Ibid., 160.

CHAPTER TEN

"Where is Everybody?" Leading Worship in a Small Group or Church Plant

WHERE IS EVERYBODY?

In a small group or a church plant, chances are good that people are coming to the gathering with the sense of "we're not all here." The small group is keenly aware that Sunday morning is when everyone gathers, but this event is only a small piece of the whole. The church plant has vivid memories of being in an established church that seemed to have it all (not that you felt that when you were there!). However it confronts us, the feeling can be there that we don't have enough people to accomplish something great. We can say a few things about that.

First, we can say that it only takes "two or three." When Jesus was speaking on how to address unrepentant sin in a local church he told us something that has far-reaching implications: "Where two or three are gathered in my name, there am I among them" (Matt. 18:20). This does not mean that the "two or three" are a complete church, but merely that Christ is present. And if God is present, then he is there in all of his power, glory, grace, truth, love, and presence.

Second, we should remember that where Christians are, the gifts of the Spirit are: "To each is given the manifestation of the Spirit for the common good" (1 Cor. 12:7). "But grace was given to each one of us according to the measure of Christ's gift" (Eph. 4:7). This means that while *all* the gifts might not be represented, every person gathered has gifts that God has given to serve and bless others.

Third, if a gathering is indeed a church—and a church means there is an elder to lead it, an ongoing practice of the sacraments, a commitment to church discipline, etc.—then it is a church. When Luke was describing Paul and Barnabas ministering in a certain city he would say things like "they met with the church and taught a great many people" (Acts 11:26); or, "When he had landed at Caesarea, he went up and greeted the church" (18:22). The significance here is that these smaller churches are true churches. These smaller fellowships would have been dwarfed by the church in Jerusalem, but they are still regarded as complete churches. They might be young and small, but they are true churches, and as a true church they have all the gifts they need to thrive, grow, and experience the presence of God.

These three points should give us great faith as we gather. God's people are there, and God himself is there! God's gifts are present, and they are enough to experience great things. Whether we are meeting as a small group of a larger church or a church plant, let us come to that gathering with great faith.

TWO SERMONS TO PREACH TO YOURSELF

There are two sermons that worship leaders need to get really good at preaching to themselves. Whether you lead for your family or a 15,000-member church, they are probably two sermons to have virtually memorized. The first one is called, *"It's not about me."* A sinful heart sees the priceless but quickly gets distracted by the worthless. We leave the treasure hidden in the field and go after the thorn bush in the forest. With worship what that means is that we develop a song list of God-centered songs, find a God-centered Scripture, think about a God-centered response to these, and then somewhere along the line we begin to think that *how we do* at this given task is more important than *who God is*. In other words, worship becomes "about me" instead of being "about God." It's good to preach to yourself that whether we mess up or play perfectly, whether we sing out-of-tune or the songs of angels, whether no one participates in our "great idea" or revival breaks out, we are good with it because worship is about God, not us.

The second sermon to preach to yourself often is a related one: *"It's not up to me."* In other words, the spiritual impact of a time of corporate worship is something God has to do. A verse that has captured this vividly for me over the years is John 15:5: "I am the vine; you are the branches. Whoever abides in me and I in him, he it is that bears much fruit, for apart from me you can do nothing." Note how absolute Jesus' word is: "nothing" (the Greek is as absolute as the English here). If "nothing" is possible for you apart from Christ, how could corporate worship ever be up to you? Yes, you must prepare faithfully, pray faithfully, and lead as effectively as you can. But in the end, if God doesn't show up, nothing will happen.

Think of what this earth was before God acted in the six days of Creation. The Bible says it was "formless," "void," and covered in "darkness" (Gen. 1:2). All of this changed when God spoke the language of Creation: "Let there be...and there was" (1:3). This might sound overly dramatic for your small group meeting, but the point is no less true there. Without God's power, you are "formless," "void," and covered in "darkness." But if God acts through his Spirit, there will be form, fullness, and brilliant light!

So, it's not about you and it's not up to you. Those points should inform our prayers and faith for worship. They should inform our anxiety. They should inform our peace before a time of worship. Learn these two sermons well and preach them often.

IT'S HARDER AND DIFFERENT

The need for faith should not make us naïve about leading a smaller group in worship. The truth is, it's a lot harder. Generally it takes much more work by the worship leader than the typical Sunday meeting of an established church. One reason for this is expectations. People do not come to a Wednesday night home fellowship with the same sense of expectation that they do on a Sunday morning. On Sunday they might expect to encounter God and be confronted by his Word. Yet, on a Wednesday night they are just looking to be encouraged and to connect with some believers they love. This affects the worship because people won't generally be quite as energetic, expectant, or even engaged.

In a church plant, it is a Sunday service, but the smaller size and more limited abilities of people often mean that people simply expect less. This affects their worship as well. They will sing, pray, and step out in spiritual gifts, but maybe overall they will not be as focused as in a conference or larger church setting. This makes the role of the worship leader more difficult.

Related to this, with the smaller setting you are often dealing with people new to the church or your style of church. There is no cadre of people who have been there for years and who are comfortable with and knowledgeable about how you do things. That means it might be necessary to remind people even weekly of what to expect and what to pursue during your time together. If you have a 'prophecy mic' in the front, remind people of that and encourage them about bringing Scriptures, prophecies, or even tongues and interpretations. If you will be taking the Lord's Supper, let people know it's coming and when to expect it.

But along with this difficulty is the real sense in which it is simply different. When I go to a church plant I am expecting a very relational experience and to be a part of something undeveloped and establishing itself. I might be a bit less engaged during the worship, but before and after the meeting I soak in the friendships being developed. Maybe the overall corporate worship experience is less intense than in other contexts, but my joy at being part of such a church might be every bit as great or even greater.

At a practical level, with a Sunday meeting in a larger church, often the music can begin without any introduction. The music starts and people jump into the singing. Enough people know the routine that those who don't will not be noticed. In a small group, people are just barely off of work or dinner, and getting there was a heroic effort. It's night-time and fatigue is setting in. There's no huge sound system to block out the background noise, so the children are heard and everyone's "almost-in-tune" singing is part of the milieu.

Such an atmosphere means that part of the role of the worship leader is to guide people from the distractions of the day to a moment of delighting in Jesus Christ. Maybe this won't be a life-changing experience for them, but we can at least give them a clear reason to worship Christ and songs to help them do that. Here it can be difficult to start with singing because of our distracted thoughts. Help people to focus on the Lord first, and then turn to the singing. Of course, prayer is a great way to settle anxious souls.

In this sense, there is much more deliberate "shepherding" in a small setting or church plant. As much as you can, try and identify with where the people are—who haven't been praying about or thinking about this time of worship for a couple days like you have, or even a couple seconds. Their goal was to get there, and they did. You need to take them at this state of heart and guide them to a time of worshiping their Savior.

CAPITALIZE ON YOUR SIZE

Every sized fellowship offers opportunities, and we should work to capitalize on them. The gold mine for the smaller group is relationship. If relationship is not happening in the smaller setting, then you are missing out on the greatest asset you have.

A smaller size also means less pressure and risk. Stepping out in the area of spiritual gifts in a large church can be intimidating, but doing it in a small group presents far fewer hurdles (still hurdles, but smaller). In a smaller meeting you can afford to have someone read the Bible out loud who doesn't do it very well.

A church plant has a similar dynamic with relationship being the great asset it has. That will be the essential ingredient that will enable people to tolerate a mountain of imperfections. A competing factor in the church plant is its desire to grow, which typically means that we cannot afford all the risks of a home small group. Yet, part of long-term growth also includes giving some people experience at things where they are merely okay so that one day they will be very effective. A church plant provides numerous opportunities for that kind of on-the-job training.

The smaller context of a church plant also means you can structure worship at times in a very practical "how-to" manner. Begin with a song and then give explanation about a specific practice from the Psalms or the New Testament. Then allow time to do that practice. This type of practical instruction feels odd in a large gathering, but in a small one (under 150 people), it can be edifying and helpful.

BE A WORSHIPER

Our personal integrity as a worshipper becomes even more important in a smaller setting like a church plant or home fellowship. Some of this is the practical reality of people knowing us better. Whoever we are becomes part of how people receive our leadership. Thus, our heart as a worshiper and our example of worshiping will have an even greater impact in a small group. Preserving a worshipful and quiet heart can be difficult in a small setting where distractions seem even more distracting—mistakes, crying babies, awkward layouts, people coming and going. We will likely have to work harder to maintain a settled soul and a mind that is engaging God.

Of course, along with these encouragements we should remember that we can afford to be more natural. A larger setting often means you need to act bigger, speak bigger, and think bigger. You're shepherding a much larger group. The smaller setting means we can be less formal and more ourselves. In fact, in the small setting we want to avoid people having the reaction, *"Where does he think he is? Doesn't he realize there's only 20 of us?"*

KEEP IT SIMPLE

Perhaps you have heard of the "K-I-S-S" method of doing things: "Keep it simple, stupid." Leading worship in a small group or church plant is one place to keep this in mind. In a large church people expect more creativity, diversity, and a greater representation of the possibilities. In a small group, they are content with a more routine approach. This doesn't mean putting a stop to creativity, but remembering that the need is slightly less in a smaller context.

For instance, song lists in a larger setting need to pull from a greater number of songs and be more varied in the flow of the set. In a smaller setting, it is often effective to adopt a C-2-1 approach. That simply means beginning with a call to worship (C) that gives people a reason to worship Christ at that moment. Then do two (2) fast songs (or medium tempo) and end with one (1) slow song.

Fast songs help in a small group that is likely meeting in the evening, because slow reflection and end of the workday often do not go well together! Fast songs also tend to pull people out of themselves more easily, and this is helpful if we are wanting to incorporate spiritual gifts in our worship times.

In a church plant you will be doing more songs and the creative elements need to have a greater place, but keeping it simple is still important. Perhaps special music and/or choirs is a way to apply this. Special music in a larger church is more assumed and more possible because of the larger pool of talent. In a smaller setting, special music can often prove difficult. The band is barely able to get enough musicians for each Sunday without killing them, so adding special music to a meeting can be far more effort than it's worth. Be content to keep that on the shelf until the church grows and people have more room in their schedules.

How much simplicity and how much creativity are issues the leader must decide upon. I am only suggesting here that we should not feel too much pressure to add creativity that is simply beyond our basic abilities. Doing something heroic for your Christmas Eve service or Easter service is one thing because it's once in the year. What we need to guard ourselves against is trying to add this kind of heroic effort too often. When in doubt, choose simplicity over creativity, and let God bring the creativity at a later date.

LOVE YOUR PEOPLE

The call to love our brothers and sisters in Christ is not reserved for leaders or non-leaders, pastors or volunteers, big churches or small groups. It is for all of us. Jesus commanded us to "love one another: just as I have loved you, you also are to love one another" (John 13:34). In fact, it is by this one action that "all people will know that you are my disciples, if you have love for one another" (v. 35). How does this relate to our topic at hand? We can say a couple things.

Love for our brothers and sisters helps us to *identify* with them. They are not generic people we happen to be leading in worship. They are specific people that we identify with. Their struggles are our struggles; their joys are our joys; their experiences are our experiences. This means that we feel their pain and joy to an extent, and also that we truly, deeply feel that we are one of them. This kind of identification is part of Christian love: "Rejoice with those who rejoice, weep with those who weep" (Rom. 12:15).

Love for our brothers and sisters also provokes us to *know* them. Without love we are tempted to be distant from them, or condescending in our attitude, or less concerned about their spiritual health. To effectively lead people in worship, whether 15 or 15,000, I need to know them. Knowing them helps me to build song lists that address them where they are, and it will especially help me to craft calls to worship that take them where they are and bring them into a greater awareness of Christ and his grace and glory.

This is profoundly difficult and even impossible if I don't know something of the people I am leading. The great benefit of a small group or a church plant is the opportunity to truly know each one of the people I am leading in worship.

Sometimes a direction in worship will arise if you stop and think through each of the families you are involved with. That gives me a general sense of the spiritual state of the group. Then I can reflect on what their needs are and what will best serve them. This kind of individual approach is virtually impossible for the larger church, because of the sheer diversity of needs and life situations.

Such a response to your group is really a kind of "shepherding" of your group, imagining yourself as the shepherd in the moment who is trying to lead these particular sheep to "green pastures" and "still waters" (Ps. 23:2). All effective leadership has this aspect of shepherding to it, and leading worship in a small group is no exception.

You can see how my love for the people will make all of this easier and more natural. I will do it not because my task is worship leading and this is what worship leaders do, but because I love these people and I want to serve them as effectively as possible. When they experience God in a way that builds their faith it gives me joy because I have helped people I love. This is different than being joyful over a task I happened to do well.

Such love will also motivate us for the long haul. The weekly and monthly grind of life can make routine activities dry as dust unless we step back and remember that, *"Wait a minute, I love these people. Of course I want to work hard and see them thrive."* Another benefit of loving your people is that they will be much better positioned to receive your leadership. People are amazingly forgiving when they know you love them. Love helps us to receive from bad preachers and inadequate worship leaders. People might want us to improve, but they will be extremely patient until we do *if they know we love them.* As Peter tells us, "Love covers a multitude of sins" and worship leading disasters. Note that he said "a multitude," not "occasional and rare." So, if you do nothing else, love your people.

MORE MUSICAL ISSUES

A lot of the talk in the chapter on music and musicians will assume a full band. But, how to run an audition for a drummer is a bit meaningless if no one in your church plays drums. And certainly in a home group you are not likely to set up a band for a few songs. The smaller context should not make us negligent about the music, however. Here are a few things to consider.

1. Play loud and soft. While it is true that a lot of the arranging ideas above have little relevance for you, the concept of *dynamics* still has a place. This means having at least a couple intensity levels for your guitar playing (or piano). At the very least have times where you play loudly and times where you play softly. Maybe you play softer at the verses and louder at the choruses. This helps people respond to the music because it won't be a flat unending line of music. It will have some shape to it.

2. Be as creative as you can reasonably be. Musical creativity helps people to engage with the songs they sing, so even if our resources are limited (number or quality of instrumentalists), strive for a reasonable level of creativity. A first point to make here is to listen as much as you can to bands that have a similar set of instruments. There are bands out there of all shapes and sizes from a single guitar and voice, to the swing bands with entire horn sections. Find a few that roughly equate to what you have and listen to how they create a whole album's worth of music. Worship music from Indelible Grace and Red Mountain Music works a lot in these trimmed-down bands.

A second point to consider here is the principle of *whatever you did on the last song, don't do it on this song.* If the last song was guitar-driven, make this one piano-driven. If you started with drums and acoustic on the last song, start with just guitar on this one. I have noticed that a lot of sets that feel creative really had just a slight variation with how they started certain songs. Once the songs were going they were pretty similar—maybe everyone playing fairly strongly. If you can give just a little thought to starting songs in different ways, you can provide a good creativity for your people.

As you develop as a small worship team, allow for trial-and-error. Maybe you wanted a pianist to start the song, but they are not quite able. No problem. You start all the songs, but at certain points you'll play soft so that the piano can be heard more dominantly. Maybe you thought the "drums only" *Be Thou My Vision* would surely be a hit, and it just…wasn't. No problem. You won't try that next time. Any band worth anything goes through about fifty variations of a song before they land on the arrangement that makes the album. Expect that you're band will have that same journey.

Your trial-and-error will generally be more successful if you keep in mind certain "rules" of arranging. In our chapter on music we mentioned *clarity* and *simplicity*, but for you these will be almost unavoidable. With very small bands every instrument is heard and the arrangement is simple without doing any work. Other rules will become more relevant. For instance, when you have drums, you need to have a bass player. If you lack a bass player, try and develop a "percussionist," a guy maybe based on the djembe or congas, but who can also bring in shakers, perhaps timbales, a few cymbals, etc.

Also, with instruments that overlap like the piano and guitar, make sure they aren't duplicating parts. You want them to play *complementary* parts, not *identical* parts. If the acoustic player is banging out chords and the piano player is playing thick chords around the middle of the piano, even though two are playing it will sound "muddy." If the guitarist is in the middle register, have the piano player go lower and higher (i.e., spreading his hands further apart). Similarly, if the guitarist is banging out chords, have the piano player doing arpeggios or single-note parts.

If the band lacks a bass player and the piano player is the bass, help him truly own that spot on the team. Octaves that stay below middle-C will thicken up the low-end. Further, maybe think chords/arpeggios during the verse, but repeating 8th-note octaves at the chorus to add intensity and drive to that part of the song. These kinds of devices can bring more intensity than you might think to a small team.

Another point to remember here is that your church is not keeping track of what you did last week. They are not thinking to themselves, *"But he started a song with that muted acoustic thing last week, and now he's doing it again!"* That's how we listen to albums by bands we love, but it's not how we listen to live music, and it's definitely not how we listen to music in church.

With live music you are aware of the musicians present, not the ones that similar bands have or that other worship teams have. People are (generally) not wishing for an electric guitar player if there isn't one on stage, or for a female vocalist if all you have is a male lead. They naturally adjust to who is actually there. All of us are unavoidably *present tense,* as it were, dealing with the worship team as it is right now. All we are trying to do with creativity is to vary just a bit the sounds and intensities of these musicians.

3. Have at least two styles of guitar or piano playing. The guitar and piano are very hard to play well. Playing "a little bit" usually takes 6-18 months, but to play well takes years of practice. The truth is, you may never get there given the time you have in your life to give to it. Perhaps make it your goal to at least develop two different styles of playing. For guitarists, be able to play chords strumming and to play those chords arpeggiated (one note at a time). Those two styles can be alternated throughout the song list to give some variety to the music. On piano, the same is true. Play parts of songs with block chords and parts arpeggiated. As your playing develops you can add more rhythmic techniques, but shoot for at least two.

4. Learn to take a breath during your sets. One challenge for me and other leaders is taking "a breath" during sets, having times where you are playing quietly while people are waiting on the Lord, or someone is prophesying, or you are deciding what step to take next. An easy way to do this is to take the chord progression of the chorus of the current song and strum it softly. This can also be a time where you encourage people to speak a Scripture or prayer that is on their hearts.

5. Do songs you can do WELL. A temptation in these smaller worship contexts is to try and reproduce what you experience in a Sunday service of an established church. Part of this pressure includes doing a whole array of songs—new and old, hymns and contemporary choruses, etc. This is fine if our musical abilities and time allow for it, but for most of us this means we end up doing some songs that we don't know well. Our playing is just a little off, the tempo is too slow, or maybe our memory of the melody isn't...quite right.

Such mistakes are very distracting for people—much more distracting than repeating a set of songs you know WELL. People do not come with song counters in their Bibles where they keep track of your song lists and the number of repeating songs. They are just singing. Maybe shoot for the goal of having 2-3 months of songs in your arsenal (about 12-18 songs), but then be content to mix these up in your song lists. As Bob Kauflin has said, singing *In Christ Alone* every time your small group meets is not at all a bad thing.

The benefit of this is that not only will you know the songs well, but your people will also. Repetition gives them a chance to memorize songs and really own them. Jumping around to the latest "Top 40" worship song often means people never quite know the songs they are singing.

Just as important, people can follow along much better when they feel confident about the rhythm you are giving them and when your melody is like the version they remember. There is no rocket science here, but hopefully these encouragements help you.

GRACE IS BIGGER

As we close this section, we will let the grace of God get the final word. In 2 Corinthians Paul famously speaks of "a thorn...given me in the flesh," something he even calls "a messenger of Satan to harass me" (12:7). Whatever the thorn was—sickness, ailment, speech impediment, personal struggle, etc.—is never revealed. His prayers for relief went unanswered in terms of being answered as Paul wanted. They were certainly answered. In fact, God speaks a word to him meant to clarify what his real need was: "My grace is sufficient for you, for my power is made perfect in weakness" (v. 9). Paul got it: "Therefore I will boast all the more gladly of my weaknesses, so that the power of Christ may rest upon me" (ibid.).

What was true of Paul is true of us in every situation, and it is true as we lead worship. We bring to the task a host of weaknesses—musical limitations, theological deficiencies, biblical ignorance, a lack of experience, a limited perspective on our ourselves and our people, perhaps a true sense that we don't know Christ as well as we should or that we have not experienced enough in the Holy Spirit. At times these weaknesses have a real impact on our leadership and we know things could have been more effective with greater strengths.

Yet, God's "grace is sufficient for you." "Sufficient" means it is enough. When this word is used in other places in the New Testament it has to do with being content because we have what we need: "But if we have food and clothing, with these we will be content" (1 Tim. 6:8); "Keep your life free from the love of money, and be content with what you have" (Heb. 13:5).

The grace of God gives us true sufficiency and should also bring contentment. His favor, mercy, power, presence, and blessing are all part of his grace. God is telling us here that he will do through us what our gifts and abilities could never do. But he might do it in a way that brings *him* the glory, not your gifts or reputation.

Sometimes this means the Sundays you feel worst about are the ones where people were truly blessed. Sometimes it is going through intense personal turmoil and knowing that you are just barely able to get through small group worship. Yet, God still blesses those times. Maybe it looks like a good group laugh when you completely bomb a new song. These times are not supposed to take us to the point of despair, but they are to be additional reminders to us that God's grace is bigger than all of our weaknesses. Don't use his grace as a reason to stop working to improve, but let it be your final confidence. As Paul says elsewhere, "Not that we are sufficient in ourselves to claim anything as coming from us, but our sufficiency is from God" (2 Cor. 3:5).

PART FOUR

Specific Practices

CHAPTER ELEVEN

The Different Steps of a Typical Sunday Service

Our discussion began with broad issues of theology and has progressively become more specific. In these next two chapters we will dive even further into the details of specific practices that our church has adopted. There are some principles that we will discuss along the way that will apply to other traditions and contexts, but they will apply most directly to churches like ours—those with several hundred in attendance on Sundays and a folk-rock type of ensemble (guitar, bass, drums, keys, vocals, other instruments cycling in, an occasional choir) that use a blend of traditional and modern worship songs and usually have about a half-hour of musical worship. That is a specific description and Sundays can vary, but it gives a basic snapshot of our typical look.

As much as your setting reflects this kind of context, you will likely find help below. The less it reflects this context—e.g., maybe you are a member of a small Orthodox Presbyterian Church in rural South Carolina—the less you will be able to apply directly from what we say here. Of course, if your tradition varies dramatically from mine, you are unlikely to even be reading this book.

The first of the next two chapters is a walk through a typical Sunday service. The second is on the complex and controversial issues surrounding music and musicians. We begin with a behind-the-scenes look at a Sunday service. To break up the discussion we will think of a Sunday in four stages: the pre-planning before Sunday, the rehearsal, the service; and lastly, evaluating a given time of worship.

PRE-PLANNING BEFORE SUNDAY

For some of us the, hardest part of Sunday is the time before it ever happens—the pre-planning. Coming to a Sunday rehearsal with a clear plan, a prepared heart, and confidence in your music takes time and intentionality. There are four elements that go into the pre-planning: establishing a theme, creating a song list, practice, and prayer.

1. Choose a clear theme, and build your song list and worship plan around it. The theme we use will often depend upon how the elders think of the Sunday service. Is the whole service to be about a single theme, typically derived from the sermon? Or is there room for multiple themes, one in the musical worship, one in the sermon?

Assuming the worship leader has some freedom to establish the theme of that part of the service, a theme can be chosen based on the sermon series (often using last week's sermon), a season of emphasis (maybe the church needs weeks or months of thinking about spiritual gifts or God's love or God's power), a particular burden of the leader or the elders, a text of Scripture, a particular quote from a Christian author, or even building a set around a new song (or an old one).

Like a writer staring at a blank page, sometimes starting is the hardest part. It can be helpful not to pressure yourself at the start. Just pick some truth about God or worship that affected you within the last week and use that as a starting point. Work with it a bit and see where it goes, and God will direct you.

After you select your theme, build your song list around it.

2. Create song lists that will serve your people. The point of the song list is to create a time of corporate worship that will take your people from where they are spiritually to a time of increased faith and awareness of God's presence. Song lists are personal, but I'll throw out some things to consider as you build them.

First, use good songs. That might seem obvious, but it is true that people tend to respond more to better songs. It takes work to choose songs with excellent content and singable tunes, but the effort will pay off as the congregation responds. Choosing good songs also means choosing songs that are proving effective in your church. Sometimes we love a song and it has impacted us personally, but when we introduce it the church gives us no response. Maybe we do it again, assuming they just need to learn it. At some point you need to throw out a song that is not generating a response from the congregation. Likewise, sometimes we do a song we don't personally prefer just because the congregation responds to it significantly. We lead as servants, and this is one area where we can serve the congregation.

Second, learn from the Psalms about variety. The Psalms are a clinic in variety. We see that variety in their emotional diversity (13 vs. 98), the balance of long psalms and short ones (136 vs. 1), the blend of complex psalms (119) and simple ones (100), ones that emphasize personal prayer (22) and ones that call us to loud, instrumental, corporate praise (150). This variety should mark each of our song lists so that we don't stay in a single emotional place, but this variety also needs to be captured in the cumulative Sundays of our church. That is, in a given quarter or six months of song lists, we should see an array of themes covered in our corporate worship.

Third, be careful about too many new songs. Often times as worship leaders we listen to a lot of worship songs to get a set of good ones for our congregation. Then we practice them to teach the worship team itself. Then we rehearse them for a given Sunday, sometimes not even doing one of the songs that we rehearsed. The result is that we can be tired of a song after so many repetitions, but the congregation has only heard it once or twice. We need to remember the experience of the member in our congregation as we decide about adding new songs and throwing out 'old' ones. Many worship teams find that introducing one new song per month is just about right for everyone.

Fourth, create a progression in your song list, not simply choosing songs around a single theme. Remember that your congregation is coming to worship having just barely gotten out of bed, changed their kids out of their pajamas, and maybe even still recovering from a marital conflict that morning. They don't come to the 10am start time having just prayed and prepared their hearts and sung worship songs for an hour (typically). Create a song list that meets them where they are and then takes them somewhere. Fast songs at the start of a service can help people get out of themselves and fix their attention on something else. I believe faster and louder songs loosen up stiffened arms and hardened emotions to draw us into the body of Christ engaging its God. Slower songs tend to pull people inward to a reflective state of mind. That is important in its place. The point is to create a sense of movement in your song lists.

This means that there is a thematic progression with the songs. As an example, maybe we open with a call to worship like *All Creatures of our God and King*, move toward songs around a theme like the grace of God, and end with songs of more individual response. The content is not static, but is building toward something.

A thematic progression like this also involves an emotional progression. We might be big, loud, and celebratory at the start, but end with songs of quiet reflection. We might have two or three songs in a row that build a sense of repentance, but then end with a song that celebrates our forgiveness in Christ. The point is not to do one thing or the other, but simply to be intentional about how our set is progressing in these different ways.

3. Practice the songs so that you can lead the Sunday rehearsal confidently. One critical aspect of our pre-planning is to make sure that we know the songs well that we intend to do on a Sunday. If we don't know a song well enough, we will have a difficult time leading the team in the song, and doing the song with proper conviction during the service will be difficult. Further, it is hard to have solid ideas about arranging if we are still uncertain about the song. Most of us have limited time to give to practicing, but we should do all we can to come to the rehearsal musically prepared. We are finished with this stage when we have a set of notes for directing the band for each song.

4. Prepare your heart through prayer and reading the Bible. A last aspect of the pre-planning is making sure that we have prepared our hearts on the morning of the service. Here we can only do our best. We want to pray and meditate on God's word and maybe even the songs we'll be singing, all so that we can sing with true sincerity and faith.

There are times, however, when we leave our prayer closets feeling dry, unable, and as if God is distant. The prayer of the sons of Korah feels too familiar, "Why do you hide your face from me?....My companions have become darkness" (Ps. 88:14, 18). Here we need to remember that our worship is not about us, it's about God. Further, it is not our feelings that make a successful time of worship, but the work of his grace on his people. Last, it is not being a hypocrite to express joy, to sing exuberantly, to raise our hands *as if we are overflowing with joy in our hearts*. He is worthy of our joyful, sincere worship. To say to ourselves, "Sing because he is worthy, not because you feel it," is not being a hypocrite, it is being honest. That is very different than saying to ourselves, "Look like a worshiper or people will think you're a fake."

So, prepare yourself well, but know that in the end, it's up to him, not you.

THE REHEARSAL

The next important part of the process is the rehearsal. All worship teams are different here, and my experience is quite limited. We make do with a 90-minute rehearsal on Sunday mornings. That does not give us much time and means that as a worship leader I need to plan well. Here are the basic parts of our rehearsals.

1. Prayer and Discussion. It has been easiest to incorporate meaningful prayer and waiting on the Lord when we do this first in the rehearsal. After that the logistics drive us all pretty hard. Go over the order of the songs and the plan of the service and then take time to pray together.

2. The Sound Check. Most rehearsals have to begin with a sound check. It is important to keep this moving or significant time can be lost. Start with the drums (the one instrument whose volume is fairly unchangeable). Once they are dialed in move to the bass guitar (which will need to work tightly with the drums). Then add the worship leader and his instrument (to get an overall volume on the worship).

Once this "core" is established, add whatever is left one at a time. You are listening to the basic EQ of the instrument or voice and how they blend with the other instruments. If the keyboard is using different sounds, make sure you scroll through each of them. If the electric guitarist will have multiple sounds, check each one for its EQ and how it blends with the band.

For the vocals, have each voice sing individually, but then have all the voices sing together. You need the leader to be clear, but also to have a good combined sound.

3. Rehearsing the songs. If you have done adequate preparation then you should be able to go through each song without too much trouble (famous last words!). You need to give enough direction to each instrument so that they have a ballpark for what you are wanting, but not so much direction that they are paralyzed trying to remember all that you said.

In recent history a method that has worked well for us is to assign a "primary" instrument for each song, a "secondary" instrument, and a "fills" instrument. The "primary" instrument will start and carry most of the song. The "secondary" instrument will likely be what comes in at the chorus to give the song that extra lift, and perhaps take a second verse. The "fills" instrument takes the parts of the song where vocalists are not singing and a lead instrumental part would add something. It might seem limiting to have only three assigned instruments, but this approach allows for good clarity and space in the arrangements.

Here one tension we feel as worship leaders is between being the tyrant and the dish rag. The tyrant tells everyone what to do and expects nothing but complete obedience. The dish rag is afraid to tell anyone what to do and is always asking, "What do you think?"

Generally, people are served if you give them some basic direction and then let them fill in the specifics. Telling the piano player to "carry the next song" gives her some guidance, but then she can give it a shot on her own. Once we all offer our approach to the song we should all be able to assess whether it worked or not. We can change it from there.

Of course, rehearsal time is limited. We cannot endlessly practice until everything is perfect. The leader will likely be the one who manages the time they have to get through sufficiently the songs they need to rehearse. A mistake I have made countless times is to give the first two songs I practice almost all the space we have to rehearse, skimping on the last three songs because we are running short. When you have given a song it's time, go on. Trust the Lord that grace will be there if it doesn't quite feel complete.

4. Expect the unexpected. Because of the number of musicians, sound team members, and pieces of sound equipment involved, we should expect that something will happen in the rehearsal we did not anticipate. Maybe the drums sound horrible—and completely different than they did last week. Maybe the guitar has a buzz no one can find. Maybe the keyboard signal is dead and no one knows why. Sometimes we need to stop the rehearsal and allow the sound team time to troubleshoot the problem, but sometimes we need to soldier on and try not to be personally distracted.

Further, it is critical as a leader that we not place too much stock in our rehearsals. Our experience has been that some of our worst rehearsals are often followed by our best services. And some of our best rehearsals are followed by our worst services. A bad rehearsal often reminds you acutely that you need the Lord, and your expectations are low. You approach the service with little confidence in yourself. That's a great place to be!

On the flipside a great rehearsal can tempt you into thinking that you sound good, your team sounds good, and people will surely respond this morning. In other words, who needs God, we've got it covered. Unsurprisingly, that kind of self-confidence takes our eyes off of the Lord and puts them on the most unhelpful place of all: ourselves.

If you find yourself out of time after a bad rehearsal, use that as a chance to remind yourself and your team that God is the critical player here, not us. His is the power, his is the grace, his is the difference-maker. People need Jesus; they don't need us. This can be a great place to be as you step forward to lead God's people in worship.

THE SERVICE

The next step is the whole point of the thing, the service. The lights are turned up, the sound team has everyone live, the congregation is gathered, the team is waiting for your cue, your guitar is tuned up, and there's nothing left to do but…jump out of the plane and hope your parachute opens.

Here are some things to consider as you lead this part of the meeting:

1. The last three minutes. It is critical to have in your mind that final checklist of things that need to happen to make you ready for the first song. For me that includes anything related to my guitar or its gear. Issues like intonation, all cables plugged in, all pedals doing what I expect, etc. It also means that anything related to my monitor is ready (in-ears for us, so earphone cable is plugged in and not snagging, levels up, etc.).

Often I need to make a few adjustments of my music stand and microphone so that it is exactly where I want when I begin to sing. A last element that has proven critical for me is having my songs placed correctly in the sleeves of a three-ring binder. Flipping songs in a binder is much easier than shifting papers on a stand. Of course, three-ring binders are the "old school" solution for some who have left such inconvenience for their iPads, but they still work.

All of this takes about…three minutes for me.

2. Engage God in your heart. One of the difficulties of leading worship is maintaining our heart of worship throughout the service. We will need to continue leading the band and have our discernment peaked to lead any spontaneous elements in the service, but this is not to distract us from the Lord himself. As much as we can we want to worship him "in Spirit and in truth" even as we lead. Experience will likely make us more comfortable with the various elements of the service, but from the start we should have the goal of personally engaging God during the service. Sometimes it can be simply to tell yourself, "Just sing to Jesus." As we have discussed, worship is not merely a private moment between Jesus and me, but this sense of the intimacy of engaging with our God should always be a part of it.

3. Know where you're going, but be where you are. One tricky aspect of worship leading is the combination of being fully engaged with where you are in the song or the service, but also being aware of where you are headed. Being where we are means that we are listening to the Lord, singing the songs heartily, into the music being produced. But, because we are leading the service, we also need to be aware of the next step—of the song or of the service. Not being one step ahead of the corporate worship can lead to some awkward situations—lengthy pauses as we make a decision, times where we "zig" but the band "zags," etc.

4. Lead the spontaneous elements of the service. Every charismatic church has its own way of incorporating spiritual gifts into their meeting. For us this means a "prophecy microphone" that is managed by one of the elders. People with Scriptures to read, visions to share, tongues and interpretations to present, and prophecies of various kinds come to the microphone and share their burden with the elder. If he feels that it belongs in that particular meeting, he will give an indication to the worship leader.

The key role the worship leader performs here is in responding to what is shared. Sometimes the response is to say nothing and simply go to the next song. Sometimes we return to a previous song or part of a song. Prayer can be a great way to underscore what is said. Depending on the church and the preference of the elders, a worship leader can also lead a time of ministry where people pray for others who are affected by a particular word from the microphone. The responses vary greatly, but the point is that the worship leader needs to see his place in giving a proper weight to the prophecies. If we fail to respond in any way it gives the impression that what is shared from the prophecy microphone is relatively unimportant—tolerated, but not an actual "word from God."

5. Be demonstrative. One of the odd dimensions of the worship leader role is the way that we model worship for our church. Though we sometimes hate it, the truth of the matter is that for many we are showing to them "what is appropriate worship in this church." Are we exuberant? Loud? Expressive with our faces and body? Do we dance? Do we lift our hands? Do we shout? Do we sing spontaneously? Do we pray passionately? All of this has an impact on the congregation. This a place where people are often more affected by what we do than what we say. Telling them it's okay to dance has much less impact on them than dancing.

I call this an "odd dimension" because we have to think rightly about this. By no means am I advocating hypocrisy as acceptable for the worship leader or anyone else in church. Rather this is embracing our role as a servant and a leader in a practical (and personal!) manner. There are times when I need to not do what is natural for my given personality (introverted, reflective) because I recognize that people are affected by my expressiveness. What is my body language saying about the Lord? Am I communicating that he is glorious above all things, or that being casual is suitable when you confront the God whom seraphim call, "holy, holy, holy" (Isa. 6:3; Rev. 4:8).

Another way to say this is that we want to affirm with our convictions the physical responses of the Psalms (e.g., 47:1; 150), but we also want to demonstrate these responses. This will have a profound effect on the people we are leading. Sometimes for leadership to be persuasive it must involve emotion, and emotion gets expressed through our bodies (think of the spontaneous explosion of noise and arm raising that happens when your team scores the last-second go-ahead touchdown).

6. Watch the clock. A practical side of worship leading is what is called "managing the clock" in sports. You need to have an idea about your goals for the worship, God's inspiration in the service, and the expected cutoff time for this part of the meeting. Typically the elders have a ballpark (or even precise) time for when the worship team should come off the stage. Honoring this will strengthen your leadership in the church and in the time of worship.

Another aspect of watching the clock is how we pace the service. We need to have a general awareness of how long we've been in a given song or type of response, so that we can wisely move on or stay a little longer where we are. Repetition of a song or a part of a song can be an effective response to God's work, or it can create the feeling of getting bogged down in our set. We want to avoid that and also the feeling of not being able to catch your breath during a time of worship.

7. Expect the unexpected. To have the unexpected in rehearsal is one thing, but to face it in the service is entirely different. But when you are dealing with live music and pursuing the practice of spiritual gifts, you have such a high number of variables in play that the unexpected is sure to come. Experience is helpful in this area because it reduces that number of things you've never seen before. As a guitar player breaking strings is about the biggest inconvenience I can face, but since I've now done it in about fifty services, the shock is a bit less and the recovery is a bit quicker (and the spare guitar is *a lot* closer than it used to be). Sound issues will simply happen. Mistakes by the band are a certainty. For most of these the best thing you can do is to act like nothing happened. If the mistake is at the start of a song and reaches a certain magnitude (different members of the band playing in different keys, for instance), it can be best to laugh, remind the audience that we're all human, and start over. This is the exception, however, and typically you need to keep moving ahead and try not to wear it all over your face that the unexpected just came knocking.

When the unexpected is a direction in the flow of the service you did not anticipate, do your best. Maybe it means pulling out a song you did not rehearse (but that you know!), or altering the song list on the fly. Depending on the church, an elder might come to the stage and lead the congregation in a certain direction. For all of this type of the unexpected, you are trying to sensitively lead according to the Spirit's direction. Nothing replaces experience here, but perfection is not required. People are encouraged even with the attempt. They will likely be able to tell that you sensed a move of God in the meeting and you are trying to respond appropriately. This will communicate volumes—that you see God's will as greater than your own, that you believe God's agenda is the critical one, not yours, that taking risks for the sake of following Christ is better than preserving our reputation, that you really believe God can show up in our meetings, etc. Even if the team botches the song you pulled spontaneously, those lessons will not be lost on people.

EVALUATING A TIME OF CORPORATE WORSHIP

Once the service is over, the last phase of leading worship begins, namely, *evaluation*. Skillful, timely, and godly evaluation will go a long way toward your team improving over the long haul. Here are some considerations along these lines.

1. A quick five minutes. Our team takes a quick five minutes immediately after the service to talk through the time of worship, an idea I stole from Bob Kauflin. The sound team is a part of this as well. The point here is to offer quick encouragements and observations. As worship leaders our antenna catches much more than anyone else, so we need to be careful that this is not our weekly rant about all the ways we could have been better. Remember that you are dealing with God's people who are volunteers and sacrificing a great deal to be there. Encourage them! Ideally, you would be able to comment on each person on the team, at least their section (i.e., the vocalists), and each person on the team would offer their perspective.

This is a great time to talk to the sound team about certain specifics of the morning. It is still fresh and sometimes these weekly debriefs help you cite trends. Always ask the sound team how things sounded from the back of the room. What we hear in our monitors is entirely meaningless for getting a sense of how the whole band came across to the congregation.

Talk through the arrangements—*briefly*—and quickly decide if something worked or not. Hindsight also helps us see if we were shooting for too much. The creative ideas of the rehearsal sometimes do not translate into effective live arrangements. Maybe a key musician forgot their part of an intro or musical break. Maybe the cool drum beat during the traditional hymn escaped the drummer when it came time to do it. Maybe the atmosphere of the service demanded that we not start a song big and loud, but rather with a solo acoustic guitar. Compare notes and ideas on the arrangements as a team.

2. How was the song list? Once the service is over it is easy to see whether our song list worked or not. The clever idea about doing all hymns, or all choruses, or all slow songs, or all fast songs is now obvious—obviously effective or ineffective. We can make decisions here about new songs and whether they had "life" to them or not. Here you can observe where the high point of the morning was. Sometimes it is not a specific song, but even the bridge of a particular song. Noting that is useful for future planning.

3. Was my leadership effective or not? We need also to consider how our leadership served people or not. Were my spontaneous prayers effective or did they confuse people? Was my decision to move to a time of ministry helpful or threatening to people? Was I right to let that last prophecy go so late in the set? Was I conveying with my body and not just my words that God is infinitely glorious and I am indeed worshiping him? Did I handle my instrument well? Did we handle well the Lord's Supper so that people could engage in that sacrament with proper sobriety, faith, and thanksgiving?

These questions are all about effectiveness in my leadership. There is no need to look at each one in a detailed manner. Remember, there are a lot of Sundays coming. Focus on one or two things to keep in mind for the future.

4. Did my call to worship provoke people to worship the Lord? As we saw in chapter nine, our calls to worship ought to be *clear*, *compelling*, and *concise*. Was mine? If not, where did it lose its effectiveness? Was my reading of Scripture compelling? Did I transition well from the call to worship to the next song?

5. Were spiritual gifts evident in the meeting? Since we are trying to build Reformed-*charismatic* meetings it is critical to look back on the display of the spiritual gifts. Were their contributions from the prophecy mic? Was there any spontaneous direction from the worship leader? If the gifts were present, were the responses to the gifts helpful? If there was a tongue, was it followed by interpretation, and were these handled in a way that served those hearing this for the first time?

The charismatic dimension provides a whole new dimension of the unpredictable and potentially chaotic. Much of our worship evaluation has to do with providing sufficient leadership so that order is preserved (1 Cor. 14) but that the gifts are not quenched (1 Thess. 5:19). Often it is easy to see in hindsight whether we erred on the side of order or chaos on a particular morning.

6. Did people engage God? As a "means of grace" we are doing what we do to see people engage God and receive his grace. Did that happen during the service? Whether it was tears of repentance, joyful exuberance, sober awareness of mercy, refreshed faith, or a dozen other ways to encounter God, we want this to happen when we gather. This is something else often more evident in hindsight.

A caveat to this is always remembering that you have only one perspective. Often I leave the stage feeling it was the worst worship service since the beginning of time, only to get several emphatic encouragements right after the service. Trust that as long as God's people heard his word, sang his truth, prayed together, and heard the preaching of God's word that ministry happened. We could have done better in each facet, but we can trust that God was working among his people (and the lost there with us).

*7. **Miscellaneous concerns.*** As the worship leader, sometimes the follow-up to a time of worship is quite specific. Maybe we need to figure out how to let a woman know that her clothing is not modest. Maybe a guy really needs a new guitar because his creates such problems for the sound team. Perhaps a sound issue that happened once before has now happened again. It might be time to address the sound team.

As we said above, we are not "quality control supervisors" who need to point out every deficiency in our team or ourselves. We are simply trying to make our worship more effective over the long haul.

This is a good time to remember that the worship leader must also have "shepherd" instincts. There are times when we hold off on making observations if we know that someone is dealing with an intense personal situation. We can trust that God will give us another opportunity to bring something up—if it needs to be brought up. We also want to tailor our feedback according to the person and our relationship with that person. Someone new to the team does not need us to shower them with observations. Give them one or two things to think about for next time.

8. What did the elders think? A critical source of feedback of a worship service is the elders of the church. One way or another we must have their input. They will provide for us the most definitive evaluation of the service, not because they have omniscience or even the most insight about worship per se, but because they are the ones God has entrusted to lead *this church at this time*. For issues like how spiritual gifts are handled, or the overall impact of the song list, they provide invaluable feedback. Further, they will likely be in the best position to evaluate how effective our leadership was. We might leave the stage on top of the world because of the dynamism of our leadership, but maybe to the elders it was clear we came across as "a bit hyperactive." Of course, the opposite happens, too. We think we bombed and will never lead again, but the elders encourage us for how much God used us. Pride and the sheer limitation of our own perspective blind us to how we really are as a leader. Let humility provoke us to ask *sincerely* for feedback from others, especially the elders.

HOW'S THAT JUGGLING GOING?

When you lay out the task of leading worship in this way, the metaphor of juggling flaming torches fits, doesn't it? The number of details to attend to before, during, and after the service can feel staggering. It might help to have the "emergency list" for these, the bare bones version to sketch out that you add to over time.

For the bare bones *planning*, prepare your heart and prepare your songs.

A bare bones *rehearsal* means either you or the piano starts every song, and the band and vocalists all know the songs. Maybe you encourage the band to listen to each other because you aren't sure what to tell each member.

A simplified *service* means remembering who starts each song, and trying as much as you can to obey the command of the angel to the apostle John: "Worship God" (Rev. 22:9).

The skeleton *evaluation* means you take those five minutes after the service to talk as a team and ask people what they thought. Maybe sometime that week you shoot the elders an email and ask what they thought.

In the end, worship is not about us and our reputation. It is about God. Our mistakes or weaknesses do not at all mean God was not glorified on a particular Sunday. Sometimes they are the very thing that brings him glory as the saints are reminded of his grace in all circumstances: "We have this treasure in jars of clay, to show that the surpassing power belongs to God and not to us" (2 Cor. 4:7). And when we have that rare Sunday when everything went even better than expected, at those times, too, we have to remind ourselves that worship is about God, not us. Faith must drive us to deflect glory to God when we feel we have succeeded and to remain joyful when we think we have failed. It is certainly easier to write that than to live it, but that is the goal for us as worship leaders. May God continue to refine us as we grow in this demanding task.

CHAPTER TWELVE

On Music and Musicians

Opinions about music abound in our culture and in our churches. It is unavoidably subjective. This is no less true in the church. Some love the pipe organ and some the drums. Some prefer simple songs, some extended hymns. Some want songs at least 200 years old, others want them no more than five years old. Some want loud, driving worship, others wants worship to comfort and soothe.

The fact that opinions abound in our church or on our worship team does not mean that all of them are equally right. The Bible commands us to "play skillfully with a shout of joy" (Ps. 33:3, NASB), and the implication here is that we can have "skillful" and "unskillful" playing. This whole discussion, then, is colored by the fact that music is subjective, but that we can also identify qualities that make it more or less "skillful." What we will offer here are *principles* on a number of issues, but when we get to the specifics of any of them, we must accept that there is a subjective element we cannot eliminate. Further, these ideas are merely entry points into much larger discussions. Any one of them could be pursued in its own chapter or book. But hopefully they can point you in some helpful directions.

GOD GIVES MUSICAL SKILL

To begin, the perspective in Psalm 33:3 is not an isolated one, but it has echoes in many Old Testament passages. Many passages allude to a person's specific "skill" in a task, especially some kind of art form. The tabernacle curtains were to be "skillfully" made (Ex. 26:1), and "every skillful craftsman among you" was to contribute their abilities to "come and make all that the LORD has commanded" (Ex. 35:10). We see this also as King David appoints Chenaniah to "direct the music, for he understood it" (1 Chron. 15:16).

Yet, where does such "skill" come from? The Bible is quite clear on this. Creativity comes from the same Source as creation itself: The Creator. Another way to think of it is that the Bible speaks of such skills as "gifts," a word that presumes there is a Giver who gave them.

God gifts people in specific ways to serve others. As we read in Ephesians 4:7, "Grace was given to each one of us according to the measure of Christ's gift." Some of these gifts will involve musical abilities, and as a church we want to appreciate this. Musical skill is not the only consideration for a person's service, but it is one of them.

This means that music is part of the "all things" of Romans 11:36: "For from him and through him and to him are all things. To him be glory forever. Amen." He is the source ("from him") and sustaining power ("through him") and, critically important, he is also the goal of our musical expressions ("to him"). We are to seek to glorify *him* as we perfect our craft and use it in corporate worship. If eating and drinking are to be done for his name, how much more a creative endeavor like music: "So, whether you eat or drink, or whatever you do, do all to the glory of God" (1 Cor. 10:31).

APPRECIATE COMMON GRACE

A second point to consider with respect to music is to have a sincere appreciation for common grace. In truth, no grace is *common*. It is all extraordinary, undeserved, and unexpected. Yet, by "common" in this sense, theologians mean the grace given to all people, not just those who are part of the people of God who are also given *special* grace. In some ways it is an extension of the idea that "the heavens declare the glory of God" (Ps. 19:1). Just as constellations and galaxies point us to the glory of God the Creator, so do the achievements of all people, believers or not. A brilliant painting or symphony or skyscraper testifies that a creative and beautiful God has endowed this artist with unusual skill.

In the area of music, common grace surrounds us. As a guitarist I see common grace in the playing of an Andres Segovia, a Jimi Hendrix, a Stevie Ray Vaughan, a John Mayer, a Michael Hedges, and many more. As far as I know they are not (or were not) playing to glorify God, but their playing does glorify the God who inspires all abilities, creativity, and accomplishment. To be made in the image of God is to be made with the ability to create beautiful things, and music is a significant dimension of this.

This means that we need to 'beg, borrow, and steal' from all good music as we attempt to grow in our musical skill in the church. We can learn volumes by listening to a bit of secular[i] radio just for ideas on quality arranging. How did this highly paid, successful producer approach this song? No band gets on to the radio (or into iTunes) without a producer chiseling their arrangements *significantly*. Sometimes the dead giveaway is the violin solo played by someone not even in the band. It can be helpful to listen to these final arrangements and ask ourselves why they work.

Any immersion into the world of secular music needs to be according to your own conscience (Rom. 14:23). If this whole approach offends you, then you must not do it. Thus, while common grace is real, we must also realize that our own convictions and history may mean that we cannot listen to a lot of music because it tempts us to think or respond in a sinful manner.

THE SONGBOOK (REPERTOIRE)

The songbook of a church, or its *repertoire*, is one of the musical elements of a church that has a profound impact on its corporate worship. On any given Sunday we might do something special with our song selection (e.g., all hymns, all choruses, etc.), but it is the overall diet of the church that we are concerned with here.

We can all be tempted to develop "musical myopia" with our song choices, selecting only the ones we like from the songwriters we prefer. Often times this means we have about 20-30 songs that we choose, leaving all the others to fill in the gaps. Yet, like with the food we eat, while we might like burgers and fries, we don't want it at every meal. Variety helps us enjoy every meal we eat, and it makes the burgers and fries even better when we have them!

Further, as a church we are doing something that happens nowhere else in society. We are trying to build something cross-generational and cross-cultural. Only the gospel can truly do that. In other words, we want all ages to worship along with us on Sundays, and we want all cultures (demographics, socio-economic levels, races, etc.) to feel that they *could* worship with us. Our songbook will be one way that we can build bridges across these individualistic lines.

How can we build a songbook that helps to build our church? Here are some considerations.

1. Have a balance of traditional and new songs. The point here is that we want a mix of traditional hymns and newer songs. The great hymns of the faith are known by people in other traditions, they possess profound lyrics, and often (not always) their melodies are singable and memorable. If we can include 30-50 of these great hymns, especially including one each Sunday, we will build bridges with many worshipers.

New songs are difficult because of the sheer number of them, and the difficulty in choosing between the "modern classic" like *In Christ Alone* or *Revelation Song*, and the thousands of songs that have almost no shelf-life, enjoying a few weeks at the top of the charts and then disappearing to obscurity, the worship equivalent of the band Toto. Remember them? Right.

Yet, like all things worthwhile, with effort we can find great modern songs that we can sing for years to come. There is no magic percentage or ratio here, but try for a good blend of traditional and new songs.

2. Have a balance of songs from inside your denomination and outside. Some denominations like ours (or the Vineyard or Hillsongs, etc.) produce their own music. This is helpful because these songs generally reflect our values, musical backgrounds (at least sometimes), and theology. The downside of this is that typically no one knows the songs who is not already a part of our denomination of churches. This is less true with the onset of music on the web, but even today it remains a factor.

I do not believe the answer here is to eliminate songs from our denomination, but rather to make sure that we have a blend of songs from inside and outside the denomination. This allows us to reinforce our specific church culture, but also to build bridges with those from outside our group.

3. Have a variety of themes represented in your songbook. A church will often have its theological center, an emphasis that finds its way into our preaching, planning, and our worship. This is inevitable, but we need to be careful that we do not end up with 75% of our songs singing about the same idea. Even if the idea is a far-reaching one like the cross of Christ or the glory of God, we need a broader palette of themes in our ongoing Sunday worship. Just as our preaching is to reflect "the whole counsel of God" (Acts 20:27), so our worship needs to do this. Listening broadly to different worship traditions can help us find these other songs. Also, hymnals typically have dozens of different themes reflected in their songs. Last, this broad set of themes will actually make our central themes even more appreciated because we will see them in a broader context.

4. Have a variety of tempos and emotions represented in your songbook. As with variety in our themes, having a variety of tempos and emotions in our songbook will help us bring such creativity to our Sunday services. It is difficult to build a set with emotional and tempo variety if our songbook does not have it. Work to create a songbook with an adequate number of fast, mid-tempo, and slow songs.

Further, capturing a blend of emotions can serve our churches also. Perhaps the largest number of songs will always be joyful, confident ones, for that is how we want people to leave our meetings. Yet, we serve people when we incorporate songs written from the perspective of experiencing darkness, sadness, conviction of sin, and difficulty. Provided the intent of the song is to build people up and point them to Christ, such songs can indeed be a great means of grace.

5. Choose the best songs you can. Without question we will help ourselves by picking great songs. A weak song in our songbook is like a sore thumb. Most of the time you don't notice it, but when you do it's simply a pain. We might try to surround the weaker songs with better ones in a given song list, but in the end we are better off just pruning the weaker songs. Obviously, "great" and "weaker" are subjective issues that change with each worship leader, but if our goal is great songs we will nonetheless arrive at a songbook that powerfully serves a church.

6. Think more in terms of "fewer songs to know well" than "more songs to give us a complete picture of the possibilities." One of the realities of modern life is the absence of repetition. The "new" and "fresh" seems to get all the headlines in every sphere of life. This makes the "familiar" and "old" seem unattractive and out of touch. We need to be careful with this in our worship planning, because there is great value in having a core of songs we want our people to memorize. If they do not own the song in their player of choice, Sunday mornings and small group meetings at our church are the only places they will hear it. It takes 10-20 times of singing a song before it truly becomes comfortable enough to sing without being glued to the words on the screen. As you develop your songbook, keep these songs in mind and be content to do them quarterly or at least regularly.

As I said above, a songbook is unique to each worship leader and each church. The principles above are only to give you some ways to construct that songbook strategically and in a way that builds up the people in your church (1 Cor. 14:26).

"MORE COWBELL!": SOME THOUGHTS ON ARRANGING

In this juggling act that is worship leading, we have a number of things we are simultaneously doing. We are a spiritual leader and worshiper for the service, and we are planning strategically the overall worship of our church. But we are also an arranger, almost a record producer, someone who is trying to create a certain kind of music that will most effectively support the worship we are shooting for.

Most of us come into this role with knowledge of a single instrument, typically the guitar or piano. Sometimes we bring some training in leading a choir or in composition. What we typically lack when we come to this role is experience in orchestration or arranging. This aspect of music is where the basic melody and chords (harmony) of a song becomes music—a live event where instruments and voices come together to produce a certain overall sound.

It is the big guitar and synth that opens U2's *Where the Streets Have No Name*. It is the acoustic, bass, and lead guitar that opens The Eagle's *Hotel California*. It is the choice to use acoustic guitar and strings to carry The Beatles' *Yesterday*. In these cases we are not responding to mere melody and harmony, but the choices of the musicians and producers to use these particular instruments to create a collective sound. That sound becomes inseparable from the song itself in some cases.

All great bands in history—The Beatles, the Rolling Stones, Led Zeppelin, The Eagles, Rush, U2, etc.—were not just about the band itself working together well. They all had record producers who were able to take the musical creativity of the band, tweak it in certain ways, and then create an album that would sell millions. You can hear this if you listen to the whole body of work of a band. Their first or second albums often reflect the raw product of the band, but as the albums continue that sound is developed and shaped, often by a single producer that worked with the band over many albums.

George Martin shaped the Beatles' sounds on countless hits of theirs, giving the songs the distinctiveness we so identify with them today. Brian Eno performed the same magic for U2, taking the Edge's basic echo rock guitar riffs, and turning them into the atmospheric sounds we identify with them.

As worship leaders we will not change the musical landscape of a generation like these men, but our role is similar. We come to a Sunday morning with our five chord charts and a set of musicians. The idea is to use these instrumentalists and vocalists to bring life to these five songs. Some basic principles for this will help us in the limited time that we have.

1. Instrumentalists and vocalists each need attention in our rehearsal. As a guitarist my tendency in rehearsals is to think a lot about the guitar/piano/soloist roles, a bit less about the drums and bass, and even less about the vocalists. As time has gone on, I am less prone to this, but this is still my drift. The truth is, however, that all parts of the team are equally important. Great instrumentation with poor vocals is no more helpful than great vocals with poor instrumentation. A killer violin solo with a drum beat that isn't working is still distracting, just like a beautiful piano part with a guitar sound that doesn't fit the song. Within reason, all aspects of the team need some attention during the rehearsal.

Think of a song as the rhythm section (especially bass and drums), with the dominant color instruments (typically piano or guitar), and then the vocals. As you listen to the band approach the song, listen for each of these parts and give attention where it's needed.

2. Issues related to the vocalists (from the perspective of a guitarist). As an untrained vocalist (my music degree was very guitar-focused), I still need to have my ear open to the vocalists. If you are truly unable to do this, make sure you ask a trained vocalist on your team how things sound. They will likely be able to tell you whether the alto part is working, or if the chords the band is playing match the harmonies being sung, etc.

One of the most helpful ways to hear well the vocalists is to have them sing their parts a capella (without accompaniment). This reveals quickly whether someone is interpreting the melody differently or shooting for a harmony they aren't quite getting or simply out of tune. A good rule of thumb is to take a verse and a chorus of each song. Listen for good pitch, the starts and stops of words at the end of lines and the beginning of lines, and the overall intensity of the vocals. Sometimes you need to reduce the number of singers for a part of a song because everyone singing is too strong for the moment.

3. Arrangements need CLARITY. When you are turning to the instrumentation there are four aspects to consider, and these are in order of priority: clarity, dynamics, balance, and creativity.

Clarity means that in the overall mix of the sound there is no "muddiness," and each instrument has a fairly identifiable part in the song. When instruments start to duplicate one another's parts, it tends not to add "intensity," but confusion. One exercise to train your ear in this area is to listen to the radio (Pandora, whatever). Ideally, you would listen to a style of music with instruments that more or less overlap with what you have on Sundays. When you do that, you can hear (eventually hear) that often the instruments supporting the vocals are quite minimal. Maybe it is only a drum loop and an acoustic guitar. Maybe it is only piano and a bass line. When other instruments get added they never duplicate another one, but they add a clearly identifiable and complementary part. We respond to the overall sound, but that overall sound is the accumulation of many small parts.

Clarity also makes the job of mixing your sound vastly easier. Sometimes we get angry—sadly, this is true—at the sound team because our instrument wasn't loud enough on a given Sunday. Yet, maybe the problem was that either our sound or our part was so similar to another instrument that if they turned you up, the total effect would be painful to the listener. The best solution is for them to tell you in rehearsal that it isn't working, but we need to allow that sometimes not being heard is our fault, not theirs.

An approach that has served our team is to think in terms of each song having a "primary" instrument, a "secondary" instrument, and a "fills" instrument. Yep, only three instruments. If we have more than three on the team, that often means someone is sitting out for that song. We try and rotate who sits out for a given song, making sure that it's the leader at least some of the time. We also encourage people that not playing means that we should be singing and worshiping God with our voice.

The "primary" instrument is the one who starts the song and essentially carries the song. This will either be the acoustic or electric guitar or the piano/keyboard. The "primary" instrument needs to know the song well enough to start from scratch and jump right into it, and they need to have a part big enough to support the vocals.

The "secondary" instrument is typically the one added at the chorus or in a second verse to provide the "color" and contrast in the arrangement. This can be the big electric chords that come in at the chorus, or the rock organ that starts halfway through the first verse. Sometimes it is the acoustic picking up the song at some point.

The "fills" instrument is typically an electric guitar or violin, but sometimes the piano. This is pretty self-explanatory, but it adds the lead part in the song when the vocals are not singing. This can be at the end of a line, the intro, and especially between the chorus and verse.

The solo instrument role is a hard one. You need a line that fits the song, is clear, and is compelling. I tell soloists to think in terms of finding a "hook" for your part, a set of three or four notes that you can build around for that song. You don't want to think in terms of showing us everything you can do in a single song, but playing just what the song needs and no more.

Clarity has great relevance to the bass and drums as well. Typically, clarity is lost in the rhythm section either by playing too much or by not playing in sync. Skilled drummers can be lured by complicated rhythms, and bass players can forget the power of including "space" in their bass lines. Often a song is well served by a simple beat on the drums. So much is happening in other instruments that complexity in the drums muddies the waters quickly.

The bass player is often helped by thinking in terms of staccato notes at the verse and driving rhythms at the chorus. Staccato means hitting a tight note and cutting it off afterwards. The contrast between the staccato and the driving notes will give a song clarity and dynamics.

Clarity is difficult for a band because it requires two things unnatural in a live band setting: restraint and listening. Restraint is essential because when I get overly ambitious or careless in what I'm playing I will likely be stealing someone else's part.

Listening is hard to do with an instrument in your hands. If you are listening, it is often listening so that you can blend your instrument well—because every section of every song needs my instrument! Listening means paying attention to the bass and drums to get the groove of a song, to the overall intensity of the arrangement, and especially listening to the instrument closest to yours in its range.

The guitars and piano must listen to each other to stay out of each other's way. The soloist and the piano player (especially their right hand) need to be in sync. The bass player and the guitars and piano (especially their left hand) need to listen to what each other is doing.

We are not the Beatles or U2 of Coldplay or whatever your great band of choice is. We are simply trying to create arrangements that work predictably. Clarity has a lot to do with that.

4. Arrangements need DYNAMICS. Effective arranging also requires *dynamics,* the presence of a dynamic range within a song. This has to do with the overall volume or intensity of the sound. Maybe a song has a part that is clearly quiet and simple, and another part that is more complex and loud. The difference between these is the "dynamic range" of a song.

Effective arranging means that a song does not live at a single dynamic level, but it varies throughout the song. Perhaps the song starts quietly and builds throughout by layering (useful when dealing with strophic hymns), or perhaps you have a verse texture that contrasts with the chorus texture. However it is done this type of a variety within a song is part of skillful arranging.

Dynamic range is important to maximize the emotional impact of a song. Most songs have certain lyrical moments that are the strongest emotional portions of the song. In a hymn like *Come, Thou Fount of Every Blessing,* each verse ends with an emphatic statement. The first verse ends with, "Praise the Mount! I'm fixed upon it, Mount of Thy redeeming love." To underscore this lyrical moment with our arrangement we might be simpler and softer at the start of this verse, and then as we sing this line there would be a building intensity, one maintained between the verses during that musical break. Adding this intensity will help reinforce this line. This is not manipulating our congregation, but using music for what it was intended to do: *give emotional impact to truth.*

Dynamic range is also how we can bring *energy* to our songs. Ironically, when we stay at a single dynamic level, even a high one, it does not create more energy in the congregation. It can actually create a sense of fatigue as we work through the set. When we live at a low dynamic range that same fatigue settles in, but this time because many will feel "it never quite got going," like a car that lives at idle.

Here are few ways to give a song a dynamic range achievable in a hurried Sunday rehearsal.

Play loudly and quietly. The song itself usually provides an excellent guide for building dynamically. If the song is written in verse-chorus form, have a quiet texture for the verse and a loud one for the chorus. Many hymns are written in strophic form, repeating verses without a chorus. For these songs, often the verses build to a crescendo, or in the middle of them they crescendo and then descend. Let your volume follow these natural changes in the song. For hymns it is typically helpful to think in terms of the space between verses being dynamically "high." This will keep the energy throughout the song.

Add or take away instruments. A second easy way to create dynamic range is to add or take away instruments throughout the song. If the drums drop out to a simple hi-hat rhythm during the verse and then come in with a full beat during the chorus, everyone will notice the difference. If the piano and electric guitar drop out of the verse and leave only the acoustic guitar, and then come in at the chorus, everyone will notice. This can be done vocally as well by holding off the background vocals until the chorus, or assigning a verse to a single female vocalist, etc. These types of simple techniques are easy to pull off in a hurried rehearsal, but they can create a significant impact.

Play less and more. A third way to change a song is by simply playing less or more on your instrument. When a bass goes from staccato half notes at the verse to a pulsing eighth-note rhythm at the chorus, the power of the instrument will change the whole feel of the song. When an electric guitar goes from sustained 5ths (power chords) in a low position (below the 5th fret) at the verse to a high repeating motif at the 12th fret or above, it changes the whole song. Each instrument and player has his/her own way of accomplishing this difference, but when the whole team finds a way to do it, the overall impact is dramatic.

Play low and high. On most instruments it can have immediate impact when we vary from playing in a low register to one to two octaves higher. The piano can change the whole song when it goes from block chords around middle C to arpeggios one to two octaves higher. A violin can soothe us with its sweetness when played low or inspire us as it changes to high, soaring lines. It takes care to go low without getting "muddy" in the mix, and to go high without becoming too thin in the overall mix. But this is yet another way to change dynamically within a song.

5. Arrangements need BALANCE. In addition to clarity and dynamics, arrangements should have *balance*. This means that we have a good blend of low, mid, and high pitches. The lows are often carried by the kick-drum and bass, sometimes with the addition of the piano. The mids are the domain of the acoustic, the middle and low registers of the piano, and lower half of the electric guitar. This is typically where the most "confusion" is created in our mix. We do need some instrument to handle this part of the register, however, because this is where almost all of us sing. The highs come into play with the upper parts of the piano and guitars, the soloist, and the cymbals and hi-hat on the drums (even the snare to an extent).

Balance is a relative term and how we achieve it depends on how we are pursuing clarity and dynamics in the song. Yet, it is useful to do a quick survey to see that we have the low, middle, and high registers captured. Thinking of it in terms of a piano, this means that we have the low part one to two octaves below middle-C, the mids around middle-C, and the highs one to two octaves above middle-C. Getting beyond these higher or lower is getting to extreme registers difficult to use well.

6. Arrangements need CREATIVITY. If we are accomplishing the first set of arranging goals (clarity, dynamics, balance), this last one will likely take care of itself: *creativity*. Yet, we do need to have an ear and mind for it. When the same people are playing the same songs on the same instruments the temptation is great to do a song the way it's always been done.

The goal of creativity is important to consider to keep it in the boundaries. That goal is simply *to give life and impact to the songs that we song*. Artistic expression or exhibitionism is not what we are shooting for. In that sense creativity is a slave and not a master; it is a tool in our toolbox, not the house we are building. *Sometimes* the rule-of-thumb is that if people notice the creativity too much, we've likely gone too far with it.

A team can accomplish creativity a number of ways, but maybe think of it in terms of the individual musician/vocalist and the team as a whole. Individually, creativity means stretching yourself on your instrument. Perhaps it is playing a new style or "sound"—learning new chord voicings or a new scale to incorporate, or a new playing technique (slapping on the bass, octave scales on the piano, etc.).

Sometimes it means purchasing new equipment to experiment with. The drummer adds a new element to the kit. The guitarist adds another pedal. The keyboard finds a new sound.

Even changing how your sound is amplified can inspire new ideas (e.g., going from a direct line to the mixer to mics on the acoustic guitar, going from a keyboard to a live piano, etc.). This obviously involves help from the sound team, so we need to do this with a real awareness of the impact on the rest of the team.

Creativity as a team often involves finding a new musical texture. If a song *always* starts with acoustic, bass, and drums with that guitar solo everyone expects, then change it up and begin with piano only, bringing in the drums only in the second verse. If a song is typically loud at the bridge, take it quiet there. Throw in an a capella verse in a song that is never done that way.

Sometimes creativity needs to be more deliberate. Choose a song for special music in a style you've never done before. You will need to be careful it doesn't come off as a musical joke and offend people, and it will take skill to find a song within your team's ability if it's a new style. Yet, the exercise will help the team grow musically.

Thinking of new textures and elements for our songs is a way that the worship leader can significantly influence a team and the worship of the church. Hopefully you are generating ideas as a worship team so that the worship leader is not alone in this pursuit, but even if that is the case he will likely be the one who leads that process. A help here is to listen to a lot of different styles and try to figure out what is distinctive about that style. Is it the rhythm of the bass? Is it the style of the vocals? Is it the use of the synthesizer? Break it down as much as you can and borrow from it for your arrangements.

7. Always go back to the default style of the church. It can be helpful to you and edifying to the church to think in terms of a musical center that we always go back to. That center can change over time, but having a kind of "default style" allows you to incorporate creativity into your music without losing your audience. If they lose sight of that musical center and all they get is creativity, the overall effect will be an unpredictability that distracts rather than drawing people into an awareness of God. This is why radio stations always have a musical focus. They never play everything. Within that musical focus there is creativity and variety, but always within the basic mission of the radio station.

Our musical center *right now* is essentially folk rock, a leader on acoustic guitar or piano, bass, drums, electric guitar in the rhythm section, some form of a violin or other soloist rotating through. While the leader might play electric guitar on occasion, this is for variety's sake, and the acoustic lead will return soon (within a week or two).

Knowing your musical center is helpful when you want to create a Sunday that breaks all routine. Given our musical center, we step into new territory when we take out the drum set and go "acoustic." These occasional acoustic Sundays provide a good contrast to our normal sound and let old songs sound new. Of course, doing these special Sundays too frequently removes all sense of them being "new." Quarterly Sundays like these have seemed the best frequency for us.

TOO NEGLECTED AN INSTRUMENT: THE SOUND TEAM

The longer I serve the worship team, the more important I realize the sound team is. Unfortunately, for many years I failed to see this and either said too little to them or said too much that they simply did not understand. This communication gap is common for worship and sound teams, and often it seems there is a great, invisible wall between the two and a keen sense of "us" and "them." The truth is, there is no division and everyone is on the same team with different roles. Here are few thoughts to consider about sound teams from the perspective of the worship leader.

1. Sound teams need leadership, which means that we build the relationship and communicate clearly. Like every aspect of the worship team, sound teams need leadership. The temptation, especially when we lack technical expertise is to assume a lot, communicate almost nothing, and to let small issues turn into major frustrations. Good leadership is needed to create a musician/sound team relationship that will serve everyone and produce the highest quality product.

Of course, the starting point here must be in building a good relationship with the members on the sound team. Humility, sincere concern, and basic Christian love will go a long way to building a healthy working environment in the pressure-cooker of Sunday mornings. Further, sometimes a lunch with a guy to talk about everything but sound goes a lot further than yet another set of comments after you were frustrated by something that happened in the service.

Another key part of this is clear communication, which can sometimes be difficult when the typical "taught myself how to play" guitarist meets the "professional electrical engineer learning how to run sound" volunteer. Art collides into science, and the results can be ugly. It can take a while to learn what the other means by certain things, and for the leader to clearly articulate a vision for the Sunday morning sound.

Clear communication always means communicating in a language meaningful to the *listener.* If you want the sound team to do something specific you need to find out how to communicate that to them. For many years I would tell our sound team useful things like, "a big, rock sound." Or the equivalent of, "give me Led Zeppelin in a bottle." This meant absolutely nothing to them. In fact, unless a person has *the exact same musical tastes and background to you*, these ways of speech are only exasperating. Find ways to communicate so that people know exactly what you mean and that you know they know exactly what you mean. This takes work and humility and patience (on both sides), but the effort is worth it.

2. Take time to communicate the musical plan for the set. Part of this communication means that we convey the musical plan for the service. When we communicate ideas about arrangements to the musicians, we typically take great care so that they understand what we are imagining. We should include the sound team in this communication. Our arrangements often have implications for them, and they will be helped if they are on the same page as the band. At the very least, for each song let them know who are the dominant and secondary rhythm instruments, and who is the main soloist (the primary, secondary, fills/soloist roles we discussed above).

We also need to communicate any unusual ideas that have significant impact on the overall mix. For instance, if you plan on having a solo piano introduce a song, this will likely require the sound team to boost that channel. Otherwise, that lush piano you imagined will get lost and the congregation won't be able to tell what's happening. Or, they will boost the piano at the front, only to have drown everything out later in the song. If a female vocalist will sing alone for a verse or chorus, the sound team will likely want to boost her in the overall mix. If the sound team isn't aware of these plans, it will be difficult (or impossible) to achieve the desired effect.

3. It is virtually impossible to produce a quality mix from poor arrangements. Another lesson that took an embarrassingly long time to learn is that you cannot produce a good mix from a bad arrangement. If I give the sound man four instruments all playing the same part in the same frequency range, they are set up for failure *every time*. If I give them a rhythm section out of sync, or out of sync with the rest of the team, the best of sound systems and sound teams can do little with it. In fact, such arrangements put the sound team in the awkward position of having to cut instruments out of the mix for the sake of the overall sound. We can take offense at this, but the truth is, it's our fault. Hopefully we can catch these arrangement issues during the rehearsal, but when we do not, we need to extend grace to the sound team when they are simply doing their best.

4. For the sound team to amplify a good sound, you have to give them a good sound. Related to the above point, I should only expect the sound team to amplify a good sound when I give them a good sound. The screeching, whiny guitar might have seemed cool when I imagined it in my living room, but in a live setting, the noisy buzz simply didn't fly. They were forced to turn down the instrument for the sake of the overall sound.

I need to take some responsibility for my instrument to see that it produces a decent sound without much (any, if possible) electronic noise. This will help the sound team do their job much easier.

Most instruments have three places where the sound can go bad. First is the instrument itself. Is it causing problems somehow? Second is the equipment between the instrument and the sound board. Is a cable or connector bad? Is an effect or preamp causing the trouble? Third is the sound system itself. Once the signal gets to the sound system there are typically numerous connections, cables, and amplifiers and mixers that affect it. The musician can be quick to blame the sound system while the sound team assumes that the fault is the musician. Problems are rarely so easy to identify. Work together to find the solution.

5. Ask the sound team throughout the rehearsal how it sounds to them. Many Proverbs should be plastered on to your music stand, but one of them is, "The way of a fool is right in his own eyes, but a wise man listens to advice" (Prov. 12:15). It took years (and years) for me to learn that I simply cannot tell what the overall mix is like from the stage. In-ear monitors make the situation even worse. Even if I have the master mix in my monitor as I do, the total effect differs greatly from what people hear in the seats. In other words, I need to be careful about barking orders at the sound team based on what I am hearing. If it's essential to hear the total mix, the only way I can do this is by coming off the stage and listening from the room.

This situation means I can easily be the "fool" who is "right in his own eyes." I might assume an instrument is too loud or soft and be completely wrong. It is far better to ask the sound team how things are working. Is the arrangement clear? Is the soloist being heard over the rest of the team? Is my distortion too much? In asking these questions, it is also helpful to be as specific as you can. "Are we getting a big rock sound?" might be meaningful to you, but it's a useless question. Ask if the electric guitar is loud enough to drive the whole song or something else more specific.

6. Understand the limitations of live sound when rehearsal time is minimal. The issues above are exacerbated by the fact we are dealing with live sound and little rehearsal time. Compromise is always a part of a group of musicians in a live setting, but we feel it even more in such a rushed environment. Our "artistic" creativity often bumps into the "scientific" realities of feedback, noise, EQ, and the overall decibel level in the room. Sometimes that divide is reflected in the artsy musicians wanting something that the scientific sound team knows cannot work. It's important at such times to remember #5 above, that musicians on stage with in-ear monitors have a perspective on the overall sound that is far less objective than the sound team. We need to allow that they might really know best here. Further, while the basic musical idea we want *could* work given hours of experimentation in a studio, our pressed-for-time live situation might be unable to get there in the space allotted.

Again the mantra quoted above fits: "The way of a fool is right in his own eyes, but a wise man listens to advice" (Prov. 12:15). When in doubt, defer to the sound team. There will be another time when you can work out whether there was a solution easily within reach we weren't seeing.[ii]

NOT SO SIMPLE MATH: ADDITIONS AND SUBTRACTIONS ON THE WORSHIP TEAM

One of the harder parts of the worship leading role that relates to music is the process of adding musicians and the even more difficult side of removing them. This is an area where being gracious, humble, and kind bumps right up against our desire to place people where they are most gifted and will typically most enjoy serving. Sometimes, of course, the person's assessment of where they are "most gifted" is different from yours. Sometimes the role evolves and someone qualified at one time is no longer qualified. Church growth can bring these kinds of issues. There is no avoiding bumps in the road as we add and remove people, but here are a few thoughts that might save you from some of them.

1. Create auditions that reveal how a person will succeed on your worship team. All teams have a unique musical style and rehearsal style. Ideally, team members would be added who can fit into that style well. For instance, our team does not currently have extended rehearsals during the week. It all has to happen on Sundays, and even that 90 minutes on Sunday can be radically shortened if sound problems erupt or someone is late or some other interruption confronts us. This means that we have 60-75 minutes to go over 4-5 songs. Anyone that we add to the team needs to be able to function well with those constraints. Someone accustomed to scored parts gone over for 2-3 hours during a mid-week rehearsal may not do well on our team. Someone with little background in improvisation does not typically do well on our team.

Because this is the kind of team we have, auditions can feel informal and unplanned, but that is because I am trying to discern how someone handles things coming at them fairly quickly and how they perform under pressure. Singers will always be asked to improvise part of a Psalm over a simple chord progression that I play. They will also need to harmonize over a simple song that I sing.

Instrumentalists will need to handle similar improvisational assignments. Piano players will be asked not to use their left hands and play a simple melody with the right hand. They will also be asked to switch to an organ and a synth sound on the keyboard and play a part that works for a particular song. Drummers have to be able to follow a song they've never heard before. Also, they need to be able to pick up 3/4, 4/4, and 6/8 in slow and fast tempos.

You get the idea. During these sessions I am looking for a general musical competence, but also how the person responds to such unpredictability. Do they freeze with anxiety or can they manage the situation well even if imperfectly?

One rule-of-thumb to remember is that people are generally 20-30% better than their audition performance. Nerves kill musical ability, and auditions are a showcase for nerves. So, someone who has a solid "B" audition is likely going to be an "A" player. Someone who "fails" the audition is still not likely to do well on a Sunday morning, so don't let optimism and sympathy cloud your judgment for these. There are ways to be honest and yet gracious in these interviews. Telling someone, "It seems like maybe it would be good for you to spend a few months working on these three things before we move ahead on the worship team," has a very different feel than, "You just don't cut it." Of course, do not let your 'graciousness' bring confusion. They need to understand clearly that they did not make the team if that was the final decision.

2. Give people clear expectations of life on your worship team. During the audition process, especially if it seems promising that the person will be added to the team, explain life on the team. When do song lists go out? What time is rehearsal? How often are meetings outside of Sundays? How much practice is expected of someone? All you can do is your best here, because we all know that much of this is lost until you actually experience it.

3. Get help if you are unskilled on the instrument of the person auditioning. Early on I would always try and audition vocalists with a trained vocalist at my side. This was especially true when auditioning a tenor or an alto. I do this less often now, but it is always helpful to invite someone skilled on an instrument to help you audition that instrument. When you aren't skilled on the instrument, at least at hearing and analyzing that instrument, you likely won't know what to ask of the person auditioning. You might audition a drummer with a straight-forward 4/4 rock song and never find out how they respond to triple meters. Be humble and ask for help when you need it.

4. Learn about a person as a worshiper and a Christian, not just a musician. One of the concerns on our team is adding worshipers and not just musicians. This is certainly easier said than done, and I do not have the greatest record here. Most importantly, we want to add people who are born-again, growing Christians with a history of service in our church. We also want to add people who will be encouraging examples of worship for the congregation. Will people be inspired in their worship by seeing this person on Sunday mornings? We aren't looking for worship wind-up dolls here, but people whose love of Christ and enjoyment of worship gets transferred from their hearts to their faces and bodies. One of the most important factors for the worship of your congregation is the model that the worship team provides. This can come out somewhat in the audition and interview with the person, but it's often helpful to ask their small group leader about their example of worship.

5. Be slow to bring people on the team and even slower to remove them. The process of adding people to the team should be appropriately slow. After someone joins our church (which takes up to six months and involves a ten-week class), they are then auditioned. If they pass the audition they move into a probationary period where they are getting a sense of the team and we are getting a sense of their abilities. They will likely be on a Sunday team only every month or two. After some period of time when it's clear that their abilities and example of worship match our needs we bring them into a normal monthly rotation (typically once or twice per month). Most people ultimately appreciate a slower, less-pressured process.

Part of the reason for being slow on the front end is the high cost of choosing the wrong person. If we are careless and bring someone on the team that should not be there, we might have to walk through a painful process of letting them go. This can be difficult for us, for the person, and for the many other individuals who will be impacted by our negligence.

Without question, removing people from the worship team is far more difficult than adding them. It takes time and patience and often involves an extended process of working with an individual to give them a chance to improve in a particular area. This can be challenging for the individual and for the worship leader. The difficulty of this process motivates us to do all we can on the front-end to see that it doesn't need to happen.

Of course, most often it is a season of life issue. A single woman gets married and is having a baby, or a college student is taking a job somewhere else. These are cases where the decision is typically mutual, though occasionally we "strongly encourage" someone to take some time off. A first-time mother can assume that a few months off is all that is needed, but we will encourage her to let herself get adjusted to her new role and then reconsider the worship team.

6. Remember that there are more important issues than talent. The last issue to remember with adding and removing people is that there are issues far more important than musical ability. In the end, the person on the team is a brother or sister in Christ to me long before they are a member of my team. How I treat them and how we relate needs to be a critical concern for the worship leader. Paul said that we should seek to minister according to our gifting and even to "earnestly desire the higher gifts" (1 Cor. 12:31). Yet, above all the gifts is "a still more excellent way." That way is love. Further, "if I speak in the tongues of men or of angels [or play guitar like a choir of angels or sing like King David himself], but have not love, I am a noisy gong or a clanging cymbal" (13:1). Therefore, let our relationships on the team be marked by true Christian love: "Love is patient and kind; love does not envy or boast; it is not arrogant or rude. It does not insist on its own way; it is not irritable or resentful" (13:4-5).

STILL WANT THE JOB?

It might feel at this point like we just gave you six more flaming torches to juggle and not drop. Now you need to think about the EQ in the house and not simply cultivate a heart of worship. Suddenly you need to audition altos and not just come to a rehearsal with a couple new ideas. Though I've never been to jugglers school, I would imagine they add these extra elements one at a time. Before you can juggle twelve torches you start with eleven. Before you do eleven you do ten.

Maybe the thing for you to do now is to pick one of the many musical issues above and work on it. Or maybe look at a set of them like those related to the sound team and focus on those for a while. Regardless of which one you choose, choose something. The point of this chapter was not to overwhelm you, but to give you a sense of the whole musical package. Implementing it will take months or years, not days or weeks.

NOTES

[i] I realize the term "secular" is the opposite of "sacred" in most circles, and this distinction is fraught with difficulties, confusions, and differences of opinion. Here I mean music created by unbelievers for unbelievers.

[ii] This paragraph was inspired by one our lead sound engineers.

CONCLUSION

The Simplicity on the Other Side of Complexity

As we close this look at worship in a Reformed-Charismatic church, we have covered a vast terrain of theological, biblical, and practical topics. It is possible that by now your head is swimming with ideas, and you are utterly paralyzed by leading worship. In fact, maybe what was easy a few months ago now seems an impossibility that you will never be equipped to do. If so, I hope this last word helps you.

Mike Bullmore said about preparation for preaching that there is a simplicity on the other side of complexity that you need to get to. Preaching begins with a false sense of simplicity. You think you understand the passage and know the application. This sermon should be easy.

But, then the fog appears. You're buried beneath commentators and their opinions, you're confused by the grammar and syntax. Sunday is coming too fast. But as you press on, suddenly the clouds part and the sun appears. The text is clear to you, but now it is for real: you *really* know what the passage is about. This is the simplicity on the other side of complexity.

Worship is like that also. When you start out leading worship it is just you and your guitar and the Lord. You love God and music, and you just sing freely and people respond.

Then you learn more about theology and worship and the church and the presence of God and spiritual gifts and orthodoxy and sincerity and arranging and dynamics and....You get the point. Now you feel like you are juggling one million flaming torches. *"Where is that worship that I used to experience?"* is your heart's cry. The question is an important one.

Maybe you need to get to the simplicity on the other side of complexity. This means you commit to learning and developing in all the important areas. But this also means you commit to going back—repeatedly going back—to that place of simplicity where it really is just you and your guitar and the Lord and the people you are trying to serve. You want to encounter Jesus and you want those you lead to encounter him also. You cry out to God to send his Spirit so this will happen. You leave all the details behind to think about another day. For now you are focusing on Jesus and him alone. As Jesus told Martha, "You are anxious and troubled about many things, but one thing is necessary. Mary has chosen the good portion, which will not be taken away from her" (Luke 11:41-42). What was Mary's choice? "Mary...sat at the Lord's feet and listened to his teaching" (v. 39).

We can't avoid the details of leading worship. They are important and they affect us and others. Yet, as we wrestle through these details, pray to God to give you the simplicity of Mary who was content to focus on Christ and entrust all things to his care.

Amen.

APPENDIX

A Closer Look at the Book of Psalms[i]

For good reason the Psalms have been a centerpiece of Christian worship in every generation and in virtually every tradition of the church. They have been memorized, sung, prayed, reflected upon, read, and studied by all of God's people whether they are monks or Methodists, emergents or Episcopalians, Brethren or Baptists, Calvinists or Catholics, Charismatics or (Eastern) Orthodox. Anyone involved in any aspect of corporate worship should be very familiar with this unique book of the Bible. What follows is a kind of introduction to the Psalms.

THE BASICS ON THE PSALMS

A "psalm" is a song. The book of Psalms is thus the songbook of the Bible. There are a couple dozen songs in other places of the Bible in places like Exodus 15 and Revelation 5:9, but the 150 songs in the book of Psalms dwarf these in sheer number.

Psalms is divided into five "books" and our English Bibles typically note where these begin (1-41; 42-72; 73-89; 90-107; 108-150). The first four books conclude with some kind of doxology such as 106:48:

Blessed be the LORD, the God of Israel,
From everlasting even to everlasting.
And let all the people say, "Amen."
Praise the LORD!

These five books show some intentionality, for the first two books are dominated by psalms from David, the third by the psalms of Asaph and Korah.

There is also a kind of progression in the Psalms as it opens with the call to meditate on the word of God in Psalm 1, and it builds to the series of Hallelujah psalms at the end (*Hallelujah* being translated as "Praise the LORD!" in our English Bibles in Psalms 146-150). These observations show evidence of organization, but they do not impact how we interpret a specific psalm.

Reading through the Psalms we also notice their tremendous variety. There are psalms for private use (1) and some for corporate worship (136). There are quiet ones (51) and others more boisterous (150). Some are loud expressions of worship (98), and others are rich in their theology (19). There are psalms beautiful for their simplicity (100) and others demonstrating a profound complexity (119). Some are a mere few verses (117) and others intimidating in their length (78, 106, and the longest chapter in the Bible, 119). There are songs (145) and prayers (90). Some psalms are written for a specific occasion such as the Psalms of Ascent (120-134), and others are spontaneous expressions of longing (63).

We even find variety within a single Psalm. To modern ears this can feel jarring, as if two pieces of poetry had been spliced together. For instance, Psalm 95 opens with a call to worship, "O come, let us sing to the LORD" (v. 1), but then transitions to a sobering call to heed the word of God, "Today, if you hear his voice, do not harden your hearts…" (vv. 7-8). Often we find changes from first-person—"I will bless the LORD at all times" (34:1)—to third-person—"Many are the afflictions of the righteous, but the LORD delivers him out of them all" (34:19). Since this variety is so characteristic of the book of Psalms, we ought to see this as part of their DNA and not the work of a later editor splicing pieces of songs or poems together.

Such variety means that some ways of reading the Psalms are of little help. It is common to divide the Psalms according to their genre or type: "hymns of praise," "laments," "wisdom psalms," "Messianic psalms," "thanksgiving psalms," etc. These labels group psalms of a given type and describe their characteristics.

While this in itself is a fine exercise, it can at times blind us to the distinctive words we find in a given psalm. As an example we might classify Psalm 34 as a "thanksgiving psalm."[ii] This is well and good as long as it does not inhibit our ability to see in it commands to obey—"Turn away from evil and do good" (v. 14, cited in 1 Peter 3:10f)—and prophecy fulfilled by Jesus—"He keeps all his bones; not one of them is broken" (v. 20, cited in John 19:36).

We must also let the New Testament be an interpretive guide for them. The Psalms get cited throughout the New Testament in myriad ways, as will be clear shortly. The quotations make it clear that the apostolic church saw the Psalms as much more than a guide for prayer and worship. We need to see them in a similar light.

Further, we interpret the Psalms through the lens of the rest of the Old Testament, especially understanding the history of redemption. It is virtually impossible to see the Psalms accurately without knowing something about the way God's redemption progresses in the Old Testament. This progress includes Creation, God's promises to Abraham, the Exodus and the giving of the Law at Sinai, the promises made to David and the monarchy that endured for centuries after him, the captivities in Assyria and Babylon and the deliverance from Babylon, and the rebuilding of the nation under Ezra and Nehemiah. This broad story of redemption connects with the Psalter often and provides the backdrop for hundreds of references and passages.

The Psalms have a profound simplicity about them. Of course, this is light years from *simplistic*, which means you are naively missing the complexity of something. Their simplicity is in the perspective that it's really me, God, my enemies, and my situation. But especially it is God and me, with a particular emphasis on God. They are always utterly rooted in this world, but equally fixed on God as our Rock, our Shield, our Strength, our Joy, our Treasure, our Eternal Creator and Redeemer.

This simplicity carries over to the language. Every sentence is clearly subject-verb-object. "Holy is he." "Give thanks to him." "He spoke, and it was done." The sentences do not get lost in qualifiers, parentheses, or even prepositional phrases. This gives them a profound clarity, directness, and earthiness. These are not 'high art' which loves its self-absorbed and self-aware questioning. These are heart cries. And how simple and direct is the cry of the heart! There is here a lesson to be learned for our prayers. Make them simple, direct, honest, and blissfully unaware of self.

Having covered these basics we are now ready to work through five key aspects of the Psalms.

FIVE KEY ASPECTS OF THE PSALMS

First, the Psalms contain a witness to Jesus Christ to prepare us for his coming. Throughout the New Testament Jesus and the apostles point to the Psalms to demonstrate that Jesus is indeed the Christ, the promised Messiah. Psalm 16:10 says, "For you will not abandon my soul to Sheol, or let your holy one see corruption," and the apostles cite this passage in Acts 13:35 as evidence that the Christ will be resurrected. Psalm 110:1 opens with, "the LORD says to my Lord," and Jesus will point to this text in his teaching to show that even in the Psalms there is a hint of the Son *of God* to come (Matt. 22:44; Mark 12:36; Luke 20:42; Acts 2:34-35). Psalm 45:6-7 says,

> *Your throne, O God, is forever and ever.*
> *The scepter of your kingdom is a scepter of uprightness;*
> *you have loved righteousness and hated wickedness.*
> *Therefore God, your God, has anointed you*
> *with the oil of gladness beyond your companions.*

The author of Hebrews sees this as a prophecy regarding the Son of God (1:8-9). There are more passages we could cite such as 22:1, 118:22, and 118:26, but these illustrate the point well enough. Truly, "everything written about [Jesus] in the Law of Moses and the Prophets and the Psalms must be fulfilled" (Luke 24:44).

There is a more subtle way that the Psalms prepare us for his coming as well. There are places in the Psalms that make almost no sense apart from the person and work of Christ. When Psalm 15 asks rhetorically, "O LORD, who shall sojourn in your tent? Who shall dwell on your holy hill?" (v. 1) it answers this question by saying, "He who walks blamelessly" (v. 2). Yet, Paul is quite clear in Romans 3 where he cites Psalm 14, "there is none who does good, not even one" (v. 3, cited Rom. 3:12). It is the perfect obedience of Christ that enables us to make sense of this. He is the one who is "blameless" in Psalm 15:2 so that those who are categorically evil (Ps. 14:1-4) can "dwell on your holy hill" (Ps. 15:1). In other words, the gospel is foreshadowed in the Psalms, and Jesus Christ is that gospel.

DEVOTION TO INSPIRE

Second, the Psalms contain devotion to inspire our affections. Within the Psalms we discover what true devotion looks like amidst a busy and distracted and even tormented life. It challenges us with a fierce single-mindedness meant to prick our hearts and draw us back to God himself. "Whom have I in heaven but you? And there is nothing on earth that I desire besides you" (73:25). "You make known to me the path of life; in your presence there is fullness of joy; at your right hand are pleasures forevermore" (16:11).

At the same time there is nothing naïve or sentimental about the devotion we find. It is brutally honest about life in this world. When David asks, "How long, O LORD? Will you forget me forever? How long will you hide your face from me?" (13:1), this is not a setup to provide the pat answer. This is a man wrestling to see God's hand in the midst of a crisis. The evidence of God's goodness has seemingly evaporated, and we witness the struggle to find faith. Ultimately he will say, "I have trusted in your steadfast love; my heart shall rejoice in your salvation. I will sing to the LORD, because he has dealt bountifully with me" (vv. 5-6). He has found faith, but not by ignoring the crisis.

Every human emotion is presented in the Psalms from tears to terror, from vice to victory. The devotion they contain is not the proverbial "mountain top" emotion that comes and goes in a moment. Instead we are challenged to long for the Lord in plenty and in want, in crisis and in comfort, in our youth and in our old age, in our marriages and parenting and vocations, in the wee hours of the morning and in the heat of the noonday sun. At all times and in all states of our soul, we are to turn to God "as a deer pants for flowing streams...My soul thirsts for God, for the living God. When shall I come and appear before God?" (42:1-2).

Finally, these old covenant saints model for us a devotion that should be even more acute for those of us who live on this side of the cross:

> *These poets knew far less reason than we for loving God. They did not know that he offered them eternal joy; still less that he would die to win it for them. Yet they express a longing for him, for his mere presence, which comes only to the best Christians or to Christians in their best moments. They long to live all their days in the temple so that they may constantly see 'the fair beauty of the Lord' (Ps 27:1). Their longing to go up to Jerusalem and 'appear before the presence of God' is like a physical thirst (Ps 42). From Jerusalem his presence flashes out in 'in perfect beauty' (Ps 50:2). Lacking that encounter with him, their souls are parched like a waterless countryside (Ps 63:2).*[iii]

EXAMPLES OF AND COMMANDS TO WORSHIP

Third, the Psalms offer both compelling examples of worship and commands to worship. For good reason the church throughout its history has turned to the Psalms for instruction in worship. Psalms are read as calls to worship and as a vital part of a liturgy. Some church movements are even marked by "psalmody," which means that they will exclusively sing arrangements of psalms. Such attention to the Psalms is certainly warranted, for worship features prominently throughout the Psalter.

As we have already indicated, David's rich culture of worship instituted much that is not "fulfilled" by the work of Christ. We read of choirs and instrumentalists and elaborate provision for the people of God in their temple worship (1 Chron. 15 et al). In fact, David more than any other figure established that the people of God would be a singing people, and even after the temple is destroyed and fulfilled by Christ, the singing continues.

Thus even Paul exhorts us to "address one another in psalms and hymns and spiritual songs, singing and making melody to the Lord with your heart" (Eph. 5:19; cf. Col. 3:16). Further, the saints in heaven are seen again and again lifting their voices in song throughout the book of Revelation. As one example among many we can look at 5:9, "And they sang a new song, saying, 'Worthy are you to take the scroll and to open its seals, for you were slain, and by your blood you ransomed people for God from every tribe and language and people and nation.'"

Psalms like 150 come to us as a profound call to worship. The six short verses of this song have one unmistakable burden: "Praise the LORD!" God is described in verse 1, his deeds in verse 2, and then verses 3-6 tell us *how* the people of God are to worship him:

> *Praise him with trumpet sound;*
> *praise him with lute and harp!*
> 4 *Praise him with tambourine and dance;*
> *praise him with strings and pipe!*
> 5 *Praise him with sounding cymbals;*
> *praise him with loud clashing cymbals!*
> 6 *Let everything that has breath praise the LORD!*
> *Praise the LORD!*

Certainly the original context was the temple. Yet, the use of these varied instruments and expressions of worship is surely not fulfilled by Christ so that we would no longer use such means to worship him. Further, while the individual instruments are culturally particular, the burden here is for the people of God to present their worship with the musical support available to us. We can also see that this Psalm is...loud! Some of us might be offended to read of "sounding cymbals" and "loud clashing cymbals" (v. 5). Along these lines, many have (rightly) sounded the alarm that modern worship can seem hollow, boisterous, and irreverent. The Psalms remind us, however, that worship should at times be loud and celebrative. Thus, instruments must never be the object of our worship, but should remain a tool to help us magnify our worship of God "in his mighty heavens...for his mighty deeds" (vv. 1-2).

As a people alive because of the gospel of Jesus Christ, informed by the New Testament, grasping the way(s) the cross has fulfilled the Old Testament, let us be instructed in our Reformed-Charismatic worship by the book of Psalms. It is God's manual of worship and should have a central place in our understanding and practice of both corporate and private worship.

PRAYERS TO CHALLENGE AND ENCOURAGE

Fourth, the Psalms contain prayers which both challenge and encourage us. As the Psalms have been a mainstay in the worship of the church since the apostolic age, so they have also held prominence in the prayers of the saints. Along such lines it is not insignificant that Jesus himself took the words of a Psalm when he cried out upon the cross, "My God, my God, why have you forsaken me?" (Matt. 27:46; Ps. 22:1). Likewise we can consider the apostles in Acts 4:25 praying to God "who through the mouth of our father David, your servant, said by the Holy Spirit, 'Why did the Gentiles rage, and the peoples plot in vain?'" (citing Ps. 2:1-2). Jesus and the apostles establish for us a precedent as they pray the words of the Psalms.

The Psalms challenge us with their heart-wide-open honesty. At times we might even be too timid to pray what we find there: "How long, O LORD? Will you hide yourself forever?" (89:46). Some have criticized the modern church for its over-use of "I" and "me" and a missing corporate dimension, but we should be careful here, for the Psalms are immersed in private affection, complaints and suffering addressed to a personal God:

"The LORD is my shepherd, I shall not want." (23:1)
"As a deer pants for flowing streams,
so pants my soul for you, O God. (42:1)
"Attend to me, and answer me;
I am restless in my complaint and I moan." (55:2)
"Bless the LORD, O my soul,
and all that is within me,
bless his holy name!" (103:1)
"O LORD, my heart is not lifted up;
my eyes are not raised too high;
I do not occupy myself
with things too great and too marvelous for me." (131:1)

Such prayers offer a model for us that we are to offer up to the Lord any emotion that life brings. Perhaps the reminder here is to offer them *to the Lord.* Psalms are prayers said with a conscious awareness of the presence of God. They are not rants into the air against traffic or life or jobs or money or the government or back pain. None of these are off-limits for the prayers of the saints, but we pray like a psalmist when we lift these needs and trials and situations to the throne of grace: "In my distress I called upon the LORD; to my God I cried for help. From his temple he heard my voice, and my cry to him reached his ears" (18:6).

THEOLOGY TO EXPLAIN

Fifth, the Psalms contain theology to explain. One dimension of worship songs that we often neglect is the way that they teach theology. In fact, all songs teach, whether we intend them to or not. The only question is whether they teach biblical theology or not. The simplest chorus ("I love you, Lord") or the profoundest hymn ("O Sacred Head Once Wounded") are teaching God's people even as they are sung. In this regard we are mirroring the Psalms.

The Psalms, like all parts of our Bibles, are filled with theology. In fact, they present to us a virtual systematic theology in the language of prayer and praise. Skimming the surface of this comprehensive theology will show clearly that these songs and prayers were not trite little ditties (you know, "a good beat and easy to dance to"), but the heights and depths of God's truth in the language of the heart.

We see in them a clear doctrine of *revelation*, which is instruction about God's *revealing* himself through creation and the Word of God (Ps. 19, 119). The most prominent doctrine is perhaps its *theology* proper, the study of God's attributes and actions (Ps. 110:1; 98; all of them!).

We find a doctrine of *creation* (8, 19, 33), and even some mention of angels (99:1, 11; 148:2). The Psalms inform our doctrine of *man* (anthropology) by presenting him as a creature in the image of God and a sinner in need of salvation (8; 14:1-3). And there is more.

The Psalms contain a doctrine of the *covenants* (89, 106). There is a wonderful *Christology* that reveals the Son of God as heir of all nations and the preeminent King (2:7), resurrected Lord (16:8-11), suffering Servant (22), and Almighty God (110:1). A doctrine of a *salvation* that is by grace through faith is revealed in part in Psalm 32:1-2 (cited in Rom. 4:7-8) and 40:6 (cited in Heb. 10:5-7). Psalms like 51 that appeal for mercy also lay the groundwork for the clarity of the New Testament gospel.

Our *ecclesiology* (the study of the church) gets treated as the people of God are instructed in their worship (33, 100, 150, etc.). Finally, *eschatology*, the study of the last things, finds its place as well in the Psalter in the theme of the Lord's return for judgment (98:7-9).

We can only skim the surface of theology of the Psalms, but let this alert us to the profound treasures they contain.

THE PSALMS AND OUR CORPORATE WORSHIP

Having grasped the Psalms in this broad way, we need to explore briefly how they can function in our corporate worship, especially as we gather on Sunday mornings as a local church. Here are a few suggestions meant to open up some possibilities. The truth is, the applications for the Psalms in our meetings are limitless.

Let the Psalms evaluate us. The book of Psalms is not at all the only place we look to *evaluate* our corporate worship, but it should have a place in that discussion. It uniquely asks questions of our worship like the following:

- *Does our worship have a variety of emotional content?* Songs of celebration and joy have a place, but so do words of comfort for the suffering.
- *Does our worship present both the deep things of God and simple expressions of our faith?* Psalm 119 and 23 each push us in a different direction, and both of these should have some connection to our meetings.
- *Do our meetings have a blend of clear affirmations about God and cries of longing and faith toward him?*

Wisdom and leadership will determine how such variety gets expressed in our local context, but let the Psalms evaluate what does happen.

Let the Psalms direct us. A second application is for us to let the Psalms actually *direct* what happens on a Sunday morning (or other corporate gatherings). The Psalms offer clear commands regarding certain worship practices and we should heed such direction:

> *Clap your hands, all peoples!*
> *Shout to God with loud songs of joy! (Ps. 47:1)*
> *Lift up your hands to the holy place and bless the LORD! (Ps. 134:2)*
> *I will sing a new song to you, O God;*
> *upon a ten-stringed harp I will play to you, (Ps. 144:9)*
> *Praise him with sounding cymbals;*
> *praise him with loud clashing cymbals! (Ps. 150:5)*

With matters such as worship practices our church tradition can become the unyielding hammer that crushes anything that deviates from it. The Psalms, however, are God's authoritative and inspired word, and we need to listen to and obey what they call us to do. Again it will be wisdom and leadership that discern what is called for at a given moment in a given meeting, but those involved with planning worship should let the Psalms inform their decisions.

Let the Psalms inspire us. A third area of application is to let the Psalms *inspire* our affections for and worship of our God. We do this when we read excerpts of the Psalms as calls to worship, as congregational readings, as responsive readings, and as the subject of our exhortations to the gathered church. Whether it is a few verses or an entire Psalm, they can inspire worship if they are strategically and skillfully utilized in this way. As with all things in corporate worship, this can be done poorly, but let us be those determined to keep them as a critical part of our worship.

We approach the Psalms from the perspective of the finished work of Christ, so there will be times when we need to explain ideas or make connections to New Testament ideas or passages. Yet, this can be done concisely and compellingly so that the burden of the Psalm is not lessened but actually increased.

Another way that the Psalms can inspire us is at a more personal level. The longing and affection for God or the way that David can turn his heart and hope toward God in the bitterest of situations should affect us individually. We are "prone to wander" and make almost anything into an idol to bow down to, but the Psalms call us to an affectionate faith that looks to God alone as our refuge and strength.

****

The Psalms meet us in our earthly pilgrimage with heavenly wisdom. They call us to a life of obedience and worship and faith no matter how dark the landscape of our lives becomes.

They challenge us to "make a joyful noise to the LORD" (100:1), not because the circumstances of our lives are pleasant, but because "the LORD is good; his steadfast love endures forever, and his faithfulness to all generations" (100:5). May we find him in the crisis, and may the book of Psalms provide the vocabulary and instruction we need to lift up cries of agony *and* songs of delight.

NOTES

[i] This chapter was adapted from a chapter on the Psalms in *A User's Guide to the Old Testament*, also by the author.

[ii] Longman, *How to Read the Psalms* (Downers Grove, Ill: InterVarsity Press, 1988), 30.

[iii] C.S. Lewis, *Reflections on the Psalms* (San Diego: A Harvest Book/Harcourt, Inc., 1986), 50-51.